Nelson Literacy

Series Authors
Karen Hume
Brad Ledgerwood

Series Consultants
Jennette MacKenzie, *Senior Consultant*
Damian Cooper, *Assessment*
Gayle Gregory, *Differentiated Instruction*
Ruth McQuirter Scott, *Word Study*

Series Writing Team
Judith Hunter, *Instruction*
Maureen Innes, *ELL/ESL*
Liz Powell, *Instruction*
Sue Quennell, *Word Study*
Janet Lee Stinson, *Instruction*
Michael Stubitsch, *Instruction*
Giselle Whyte, *Related Resources*

Subject and Specialist Reviewers
Mary Baratto, *the Arts*
Rachel Cooke, *Metacognition*
Phil Davison, *Media Literacy*
Graham Draper, *Geography*
Ian Esquivel, *Media Literacy*
Martin Gabber, *Science and Technology*
Cathy Hall, *Mathematics*
Jan Haskings-Winner, *History*
Maureen Innes, *ELL/ESL*
Dan Koenig, *Health*
Janet Lee Stinson, *Media Literacy*

NELSON EDUCATION

NELSON / EDUCATION

Nelson Literacy 8a

Director of Publishing
Kevin Martindale

**General Manager,
Literacy and Reference**
Michelle Kelly

Director of Publishing, Literacy
Joe Banel

Publisher
Rivka Cranley

Managing Editor, Development
Lara Caplan

Senior Product Manager
Mark Cressman

Senior Program Manager
Diane Robitaille

Developmental Editors
Corry Codner
Barbara Muirhead
Marilyn Wilson
Vivien Young

Assistant Editor
Adam Rennie

Bias Reviewer
Nancy Christoffer

Editorial Assistant
Meghan Newton

**Executive Director, Content and
Media Production**
Renate McCloy

**Director, Content
and Media Production**
Carol Martin

Production Editors
Janice Okada
Natalie Russell

Copy Editor
Linda Jenkins

Proofreader
Linda Szostak

Production Manager
Helen Jager Locsin

Production Coordinator
Vicki Black

**Director, Asset Management
Services**
Vicki Gould

Design Director
Ken Phipps

Managing Designer
Sasha Moroz

Series Design
Sasha Moroz

Series Wordmark
Sasha Moroz

Cover Design
Sasha Moroz
Glenn Toddun

Interior Design
Carianne Bauldry
Jarrel Breckon
Nicole Dimson
Courtney Hellam
InContext Publishing Partners
Jennifer Laing
Sasha Moroz
Jan John Rivera
Bill Smith Design
Industrial Strength

Art Buyer
Suzanne Peden

Art Coordinator
Renée Forde

Compositor
Courtney Hellam

Photo Research and Permissions
Nicola Winstanley

Printer
Transcontinental Printing

Series Advisers and Reviewers

Gwen Babcock, Limestone DSB, ON
Jennifer Bach, Burnaby SD, BC
Karen Beamish, Peterborough, Victoria, Northumberland, and Clarington CDSB, ON
Mary Cairo, Toronto CDSB, ON
Maria Carty, Annapolis Valley Regional SB, NS
Joanna Cascioli, Hamilton-Wentworth DSB, ON
Janet Charlton, District 10, NB
Vivian Collyer, Sooke SD, BC
Anne Converset, Niagara DSB, ON
Rachel Cooke, Toronto DSB, ON
Phil Davison, Halton DSB, ON
Connie Dersch-Gunderson, Livingston Range SD, AB
Lori Driussi, Burnaby SD, BC
Judy Dunn, Kamloops/Thompson SD, BC
Eileen Eby, Greater Victoria SD, BC
Ian Esquivel, Toronto DSB, ON
Anna Filice-Gagliardi, Toronto CDSB, ON
Patty Friedrich, London DCSB, ON
Charmaine Graves, Thames Valley DSB, ON
Colleen Hayward, Toronto CDSB, ON
Irene Heffel, Edmonton SD, AB
Phyllis Hildebrandt, Lakeshore SD, MB
Brenda Lightburn, Mission SD, BC
Andrew Locker, York Region DSB, ON
Susan MacDonald, Delta SD, BC
Anne Marie McDonald, Limestone DSB, ON
Beverley May, District 2, NL
Selina Millar, Surrey SD, BC
Wanda Mills-Boone, Ottawa-Carleton DSB, ON
Lorellie Munson, York Region DSB, ON
Barb Muron, Toronto CDSB, ON
Linda O'Reilly, Educational Consultant, BC
Cathy Pollock, Toronto DSB, ON
Gina Rae, Richmond SD, BC
Sherry Skinner, Eastern SD, NL
Susan Stevens, Peel DSB, ON
Janet Lee Stinson, Simcoe County DSB, ON
Melisa Strimas, Bruce-Grey CDSB, ON
Elizabeth Stymiest, District 15, NB
Sue Taylor-Foley, South Shore Regional SB, NS
Laurie Townshend, Toronto DSB, ON
Tracy Toyama, Toronto DSB, ON
Deborah Tranton-Waghorn, Ottawa-Carleton DSB, ON
Ann Varty, Trillium Lakelands DSB, ON
Ruth Wiebe, Chilliwack SD, BC
Mark Wilderman, Saskatoon Public SD, SK
Nadia Young, Toronto CDSB, ON

CONTENTS

Unit 1 — Global Citizens

33

40

47

CONTENTS

Unit 2 — Tech Then and Now

Welcome to
Nelson Literacy

Nelson Literacy presents a rich variety of literature, informational articles, and media texts from Canada and around the world. Many of the selections offer tips to help you develop strategies in reading, oral communication, writing, and media literacy.

Here are the different kinds of pages you will see in this book:

Focus pages

These pages outline a specific strategy and describe how to use it. Included are "Transfer Your Learning" tips that show how you can apply that strategy to other strands and subjects.

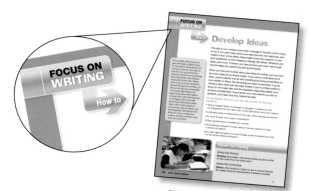

Understanding Strategies

These selections have instructions in the margins that help you to understand and use reading, writing, listening, speaking, and media literacy strategies.

Applying Strategies

These selections give you the chance to apply the strategies you have learned. You will see a variety of formats and topics.

Transfer Your Learning

At the end of the unit, you'll have a chance to see how the strategies you have learned can help you in other subject areas such as Science and Technology, Geography, History, Health, Mathematics, and the Arts.

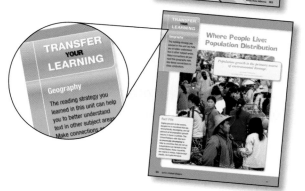

GLOBAL CITIZENS

What kind of global citizen are you?

Unit Learning Goals

- make connections while reading
- develop ideas in writing

- listen effectively
- recognize purpose and audience of media texts

- analyze sequence text pattern

Transfer Your Learning: Geography

How to Make Connections

Good readers extend their understanding of a text by making connections. There are three basic types of connections: text-to-self, text-to-text, and text-to-world. Making connections can help you understand and respond to texts in many ways: by helping you visualize, make predictions, make inferences, draw and support conclusions, form opinions, make judgments, or evaluate the text. See the following chart for some examples.

Connections I've Made to Key Ideas or Information	How That Connection Helps Me Understand or Respond to the Text
a text-to-self connection from an article on recycling to how my family recycles	helps me visualize the process of recycling and form an opinion about its importance
a text-to-text connection between a mystery story I'm reading and a mystery novel I've read	helps me make a prediction about what will happen next and how the characters will respond
a text-to-world connection between an editorial on global warming being a giant hoax and what I already know about the topic	helps me judge whether the author is credible and evaluate the text

Transfer Your Learning

Across the Strands

Writing: When you write anything, making connections to your experiences can create a richer text. For example, if you were writing about raising money for schools overseas, what personal connections could you include to help your readers visualize the situation?

Across the Curriculum

Geography: If you were looking at a chart with statistics about global populations, what text-to-world connections would help you understand that chart?

Talk About It
How can one person make a positive difference in the world?

A GLOBAL CITIZEN IS ...

**Nonfiction Article by
Susan Watson and
Iris Teichmann**

Making Connections →

Making text-to-self connections can help you draw conclusions and form opinions. As you read this list, think about whether you match any of the criteria for a global citizen. In your opinion, are you a good global citizen? Support your response.

Making Connections →

Making text-to-self connections can help you visualize. What personal connection do you make to this list? How does that connection help you visualize a good global citizen?

A global citizen is a person who

- has rights and responsibilities

- acts in a caring way based on knowledge and understanding

- relates to others within their family, friendship groups, community, and country

- develops personal values and commitments

- develops a sense of his or her own role in the world

A study of global citizenship will help you understand how people affect the quality of global environments and the well-being of others. Active global citizens do not just sit back and wait for others to do something. They turn their ideas into action. Action can take many forms:

- volunteering by giving time, help, and ideas freely

- talking to your friends

- thinking deeply

- learning more

- taking part in community events

We can all care for each other and our environment.

Global Issues for Global Citizens

What Is a Global Issue?

A global issue is a problem or question that many of the world's citizens are concerned about. There are many global issues facing the world today in the natural and human environments.

Making Connections →

Making text-to-text connections can help you make predictions. When you look at this photo of dead fish, you might make a connection to other photos you have seen. What prediction about this text do you make based on that connection?

Global Environments

Our surroundings are where people, plants, animals, and other creatures live. Global citizens protect what we have and limit the amount of damage to our environments.

Human Rights

All humans have the right to a fair, safe, and comfortable life. Global citizens try to understand what human rights are so that they can protect them.

Cultural Differences

There are many different societies and cultures in the world. Global citizens learn to live with one another by showing respect for these differences.

Making Connections ↗

Making text-to-world connections can help you evaluate the text. How does the information on human rights connect with what you know about how some people around the world struggle for basic human rights? How does that connection help you evaluate this author's point of view?

Quality of Life

Many people in the world do not have the same opportunities as others because of poverty. Global citizens try to improve the quality of these people's lives.

Sustainable Living

All people use the world's natural resources. Global citizens develop everyday living practices that help limit the effect that people have on Earth.

World Heritage

Global citizens want to protect important natural and human-built features so that they last for future generations.

← **Making Connections**

Making text-to-text or text-to-world connections can help you make inferences. What connections can you make to help you understand the type of everyday practices implied in this section?

L'Anse aux Meadows is a World Heritage Site located on the northernmost tip of the island of Newfoundland, in the province of Newfoundland and Labrador. At this site, in 1960, archaeologists discovered the remains of a Norse village.

A Global Citizen Is ...

What Is Globalization?

Globalization is about living in a global community. As a result of technological advances in communications, from the phone to the Internet, countries are increasingly connected to each other politically, economically, culturally, and environmentally.

A Focus of Debate

Many people are concerned about globalization—in particular the effects of international trade. This is when countries buy and sell goods and services from and to other countries. With the money countries make from exporting goods, they can expand their industries and wealth and improve the standard of living of their own people. At the same time, countries can use the money they make from exports to import goods and services that they need.

Tigers are killed for products that can only be sold illegally. Tiger bones are valued as medicine and their skins are used as trophies.

Global Trade

After World War II, governments saw global trade as a key factor in helping countries recover from the economic ruin of the war. They set up institutions to encourage international trade, and slowly new wealth was generated, particularly in the West.

But modern trade became truly global in the 1980s, when advances in air travel and communications made shipping very cheap. To save money, companies started to move businesses and production processes to other countries where labour or materials were cheap. For example, your running shoes were probably made in China or India, but sold by a company that has its headquarters in North America.

The Move to Free Trade

One of the driving factors behind the move to global trade is countries trading as if there were no national borders. A few decades ago, most countries imposed fees, or tariffs, on imported goods, making them expensive and less of a threat to locally produced goods. But today, every country is encouraged to drop these tariffs. This is known as *free trade*. Global free trade allows countries to specialize in certain products and services. As a result, countries can now import products—at lower prices than in the past—from all over the world.

← **Making Connections**

Good readers extend their understanding of a text by making connections. What connections help you understand this section on global trade? What do you already know about World War II and the topic of global trade?

This boy in Afghanistan works in a tailor's shop. He makes less than $1 per day. This money helps support his family.

↑ **Making Connections**

Making text-to-world connections can help you draw conclusions. When you look at this photo, you might make a connection to what you know about child labour. What conclusion about free trade do you draw after making this connection?

Reflecting

Making Connections: What issue (for example, human rights, sustainable living, global trade, or free trade) in this selection did you make the strongest connection to? Why?

Metacognition: Different readers rely more heavily on some types of connections to help them understand a specific text. Which type of connections were most helpful to you while reading this article?

Media Literacy: Of all the issues in this selection, which one have you heard about most often in the news? What sort of viewpoint is most often connected with that issue?

Talk About It

What small action could you take that would change the world?

Love the Planet

Tips designed by various artists from
Change the World for Ten Bucks

If you think you're too small to make a difference, try sleeping in a room with a mosquito.
— African proverb

Hang Your Washing out to Dry

Hungry?

One load of laundry in the dryer uses enough energy to make 250 pieces of toast.

Pick up Litter

Lend a hand, help clean up Canada

Next time you pass a piece of litter on the street, why not pick it up?

You won't get the cooties. We promise.

A woman walked by a candy wrapper on this sidewalk yesterday. She frowned and said "tsk, tsk."

Today she walked by another wrapper, picked it up, and put it in the garbage.

She felt much better.

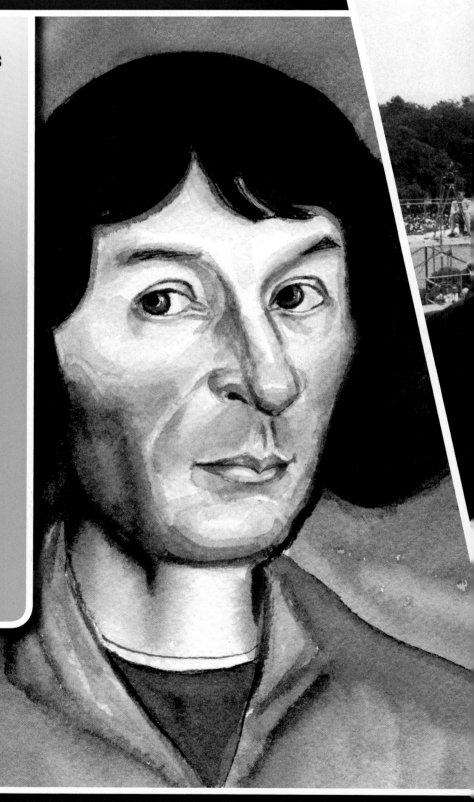

Decline Plastic Bags Whenever Possible

500 years is a long time

500 years ago, they thought the Sun revolved around Earth (until Nicolaus Copernicus, the dude on your right, corrected them in 1514).

500 years ago, Magellan circumnavigated the globe.

500 years ago, da Vinci painted the Mona Lisa.

Now imagine … 500 years from now, the 8 billion plastic bags we use this year in Canada will still be here.

There is an alternative.

It's called a reusable shopping bag, and all major supermarkets now sell them for about a buck.

Not only will using one help the planet, but your oranges are less likely to burst through the bottom and roll down the street.

Take Action

What would you like one million people to do?

One man or woman can change the way we act every day. One such man was Martin Luther King, Jr.

What will you do? What could you tell others to do?

Reflecting

Making Connections: What text-to-world connections did you make as you read this selection? What conclusions can you draw based on those connections?

Critical Literacy: This selection has a very strong bias in favour of environmentalism. Who might object to the content in this selection? Why?

Talk About It

Why do people say, "Money can't buy happiness"?
What's your opinion?

TWO ISLANDS

Picture Book written and illustrated by Ivan Gantschev

Once there were two islands, Greenel and Graynel. They sat in the middle of the ocean with a wide stretch of deep water between them.

The very first people who came to the island of Greenel found a peaceful place with tall green trees and dark, fertile soil. Their leaders said, "Since we are here in the middle of the ocean, and our island is only so big and no bigger, we will all have to work very hard to tend it and keep it as lovely as it is today. If we are careful and wise we will be able to grow our own food and learn to make the other things we need to be happy and comfortable."

And down through the years, that is the way it was on Greenel. Life was simple and it moved at the pace of the Sun and the Moon and the changing seasons.

The first people who ever came to Graynel found an island very similar to Greenel—quiet and green and lovely. But their leaders said: "Since our new land is here in the middle of the ocean and is only so big and no bigger, we will have to work very hard if we are to keep up with the rest of the world. We will have to build ships and factories and use all of our land very wisely or we will never be able to make and buy all the things we want."

There were changes on Graynel, big changes. Even though the island was small, it kept up with the world, and life on Graynel moved at the pace of the shipping timetables, the factory clocks, and the traffic lights.

Life on Graynel became very complicated. There were so many factories to run, so many clocks to keep set on the same time, and so many highways to build, that the people of Graynel decided they needed someone who could take charge of the whole island.

And so they elected Gordon D. Warden to be The Boss. He promised that if he were The Boss, then Graynel would be the best and the richest and the busiest and the most famous little island in all the world. He also promised that there would be jobs and cars and money and plenty of everything for everyone.

What he said was true. In a very short time there were so many more factories built that almost everyone had two jobs. The people had so much money to spend that everyone had at least one car, and they had so much money left over to save that there were more banks than there were gas stations. The citizens of Graynel were so pleased with all this progress that statues honouring Gordon D. Warden popped up all over the island.

Because all the land was needed for buildings and factories and highways, the whole island seemed like one big city. Where there used to be fields and forests, there were only a few tiny parks, just big enough for one or two people to visit at a time.

The very old people could remember when Graynel had been like a lovely garden in the sea; but the children of Graynel grew up thinking that it was normal to wear gas masks, and the only time they ever saw blue skies and green fields was when they tuned in to the Vacation Channel on TV.

NEL

When the great cargo ships and airplanes went past Greenel on their way to and from the busy ports of Graynel, the crews and the passengers always looked longingly at the clear air, the green hills, and the tidy little farms and towns. Businesspeople came to Greenel to try to sell some of the things made in Graynel. But they always left disappointed because the people of Greenel had everything they needed.

Finally, when even the tiny parks had been squeezed out by the roads and the factories and the skyscrapers, the people of Graynel went to Gordon D. Warden and said, "We need green fields and clean beaches and blue skies, just like they have on Greenel."

This was a problem for Gordon D. Warden. He was not about to tear down any factories or rip up any highways—that would cost too much money. So he came up with a plan. Because his plan involved Greenel, he went there to present it himself.

When he met with the president of Greenel, Gordon D. Warden uncovered a big model he had brought with him. He said, "This bridge is the greatest idea I've ever had. Your people will be able to go shopping on Graynel any time they choose, and my people will be able to drive over to Greenel whenever they need a little vacation. It will be the world's longest bridge, so tourists will come here from everywhere just to drive their cars across it. And it won't cost you one penny. What do you say? Is it a deal?"

The President of Greenel thought for a minute or two, and then said, "I'm sorry, but if you built this bridge, our people would soon be building highways and gas stations and refineries and repair shops and hotels and restaurants—maybe even factories. Before long, our island would be just like Graynel. You and your people are always welcome to visit, or even to come and live as we do. But we want to keep Greenel just like it is."

Gordon D. Warden was furious! Imagine this country boy wanting to be left out of the best idea of the century! He stood up from the table without saying a word, stomped back to his helicopter, and flew home to Graynel. And he said to himself, "We're going to build that bridge anyway, and if they don't like it, just let them try to stop us!"

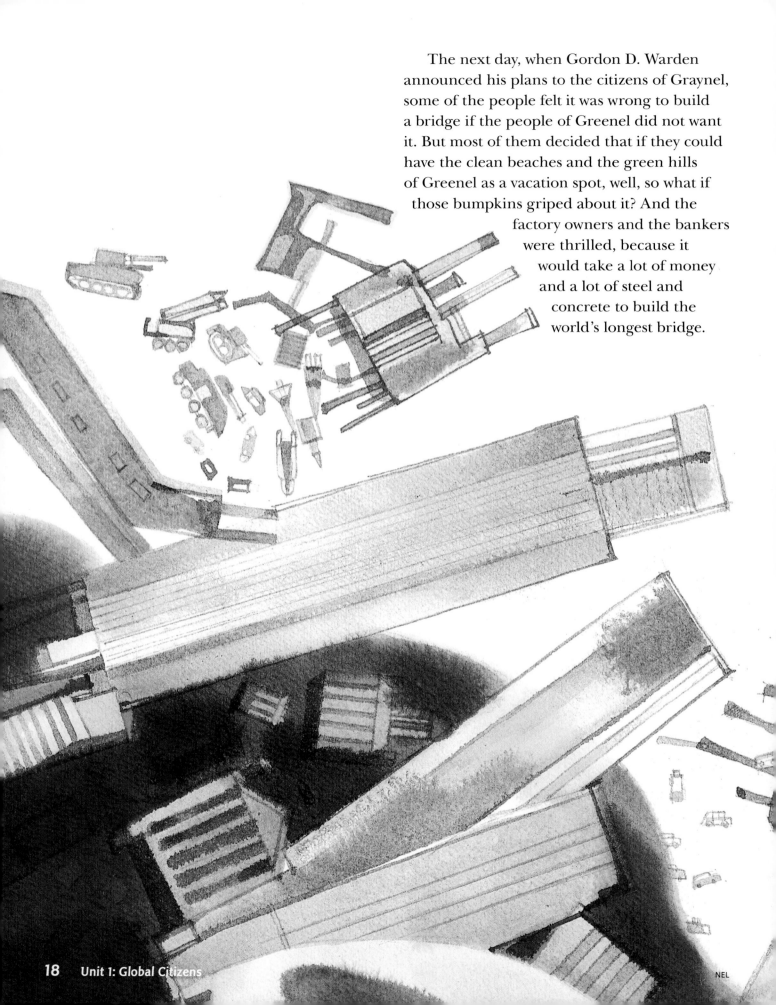

The next day, when Gordon D. Warden announced his plans to the citizens of Graynel, some of the people felt it was wrong to build a bridge if the people of Greenel did not want it. But most of them decided that if they could have the clean beaches and the green hills of Greenel as a vacation spot, well, so what if those bumpkins griped about it? And the factory owners and the bankers were thrilled, because it would take a lot of money and a lot of steel and concrete to build the world's longest bridge.

The people who did not think it was right to build the bridge protested and carried signs and wrote letters to the newspapers. They got to be such a problem for Gordon D. Warden that he declared them all traitors and gave them ten days to leave the island. Many of those who left went to live on Greenel.

All the ships from Graynel travelled to far-off lands, and every day they brought back load after load of wire and steel and rock and cement. Just to be sure that he got his way, Gordon D. Warden had some of the factories start building army tanks and big cannons. He told his citizens, "If those people won't listen to reason, let them listen to the sound of our guns!"

When the last fifty shiploads of steel and rocks and cement were unloaded on the shores of Warden Bay, there was a huge rally to celebrate the first day of construction. The Boss had announced that he would come and throw the first stone into the sea to signal the start of work.

Gordon D. Warden arrived in a clattery cloud of dust and exhaust. The people all began to jump up and down, yelling, "Speech! Speech! Speech!" He raised his arms to signal for silence, and a great hush settled over the crowd.

Just as Gordon D. Warden started to speak, there was a deep, shaking rumbling sound, as if a huge thunderstorm were caught inside a cave.

Crashes and screams, splashes and cracks and crumbling! Hissing steam and popping bubbles … and then silence.

In less than a minute, the whole island of Graynel had tipped up on its edge and slid down into the oily brown water of Warden Bay. Gordon D. Warden, the heavy building materials, the weapons, and all the people and cars and factories and everything else went straight to the bottom of the sea.

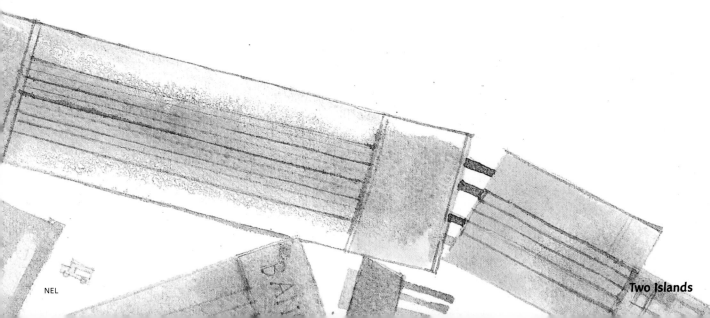

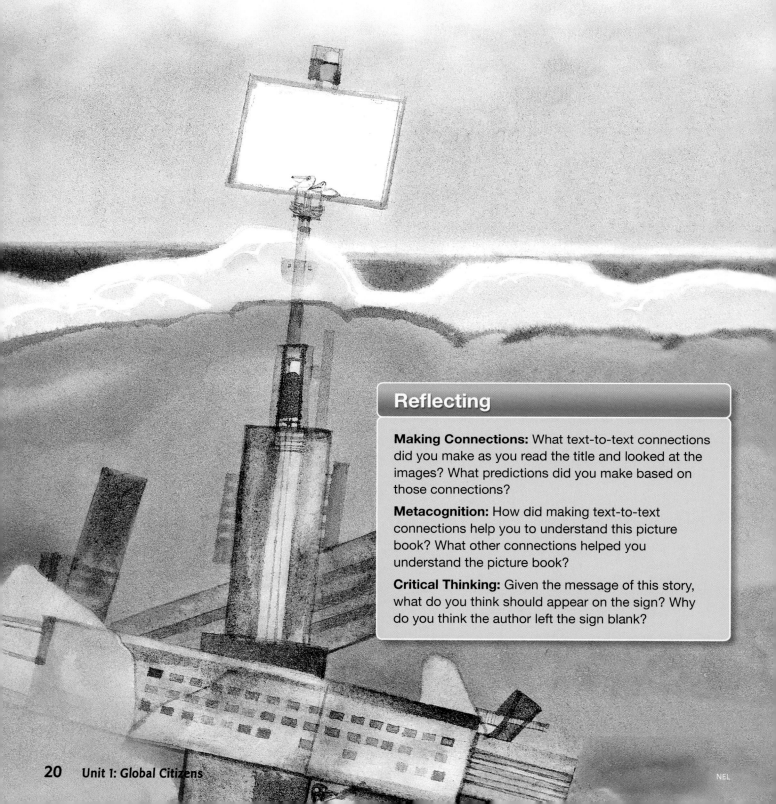

Using an old, old map, Graynel can still be found. There is no noise now, no smoke, no busy port with fleets of ships. All that remains is one lone chimney, sticking up out of the sea. The people of Greenel have fastened a sign to it, and anyone who travels past in a boat can read what the sign says.

Reflecting

Making Connections: What text-to-text connections did you make as you read the title and looked at the images? What predictions did you make based on those connections?

Metacognition: How did making text-to-text connections help you to understand this picture book? What other connections helped you understand the picture book?

Critical Thinking: Given the message of this story, what do you think should appear on the sign? Why do you think the author left the sign blank?

Talk About It
Is the world here to help you, or are you here to help the world?

It Takes a Village

Poems and Quotations
from various sources

Who Made a Mess?

Poem by Steve Turner

Who made a mess of the planet
And what's that bad smell in the breeze?
Who punched a hole in the ozone
And who took an axe to my trees?

Who sprayed the garden with poison
While trying to scare off a fly?
Who streaked the water with oil slicks
And who let my fish choke and die?

Who tossed that junk in the river
And who stained the fresh air with fumes?
Who tore the fields with a digger
And who blocked my favourite views?

Who's going to tidy up later
And who's going to find what you've lost?
Who's going to say that they're sorry
And who's going to carry the cost?

You have brains in your head.
You have feet in your shoes.
You can steer yourself
Any direction you choose.
— Dr. Seuss

Family

Poem by Carl Sandburg

There is only one man in the world
and his name is All Men.
There is only one woman in the world
and her name is All Women.
There is only one child in the world
and the child's name is All Children.

A candle loses nothing of its
light by lighting another candle.
— James Keller

We cannot live for ourselves alone.
Our lives are connected by a
thousand invisible threads, and
along these sympathetic fibres,
our actions run as causes and
return to us as results.
— Herman Melville

Snowflakes are one of nature's
most fragile things, but just
look what they can do when
they stick together.
— Verna M. Kelly

I'd Like to Squeeze

Poem by John Agard

I'd like to squeeze this round world
into a new shape

I'd like to squeeze this round world
like a tube of toothpaste

I'd like to squeeze this round world
fair and square

I'd like to squeeze it and squeeze it
till everybody had an equal share

Reflecting

Making Connections: Think of the text-to-world connections you made as you read one of these poems or quotations. What conclusions did you draw?

Metacognition: Which of these poems or quotations did you connect most strongly to? How did making a strong connection help you understand that selection?

Critical Thinking: Choose two of the authors in this selection. What would they say to each other about being a good global citizen? How would those authors answer the question in the Talk About It on page 21?

How to ➤ # Develop Ideas

The idea in your writing is your main message or the story you're trying to tell. If you aren't clear about your idea from the very beginning, your readers never will be either. Ideas might come from research or your own experience, or from reading or talking with others. Wherever your ideas come from, however, you have to know your topic well enough that the ideas you present are strong and sound.

When you first start to think about your ideas for writing, you may have too many ideas or too broad a topic. If you were to write about all of them, you'd probably end up with something too long and rambling for your readers to follow. So narrowing your topic is important. If you're writing a story, stick with the major events. If you're writing nonfiction, focus on one major idea and the important supporting details, such as facts and examples. If you narrow your topic before you start to research, you'll also have less material to read.

As you develop and focus your idea, ask yourself the following questions:

- What is my topic? What's the message or main idea? Is it clear to me what I'm writing about? (If it isn't clear to you, it's NOT going to be clear to your readers!)

- Is that topic narrow enough to focus on? How can I narrow that topic even further?

- Do I know the topic well enough to write about it?

- What supporting facts or examples can I include?

- What information shouldn't I include, because it will just overload my writing or distract my readers?

- Do I return again and again to my main message, so that my readers know what it is from the first sentence to the last?

For example, Stevie has been given the topic of global issues to write about. Immediately, she chooses to narrow that topic so that she can concentrate her research and focus on something that interests her.. She chooses sustainable living. After doing a bit of research, she decides to narrow the topic even further, to the use of water in a sustainable community. She finds great supporting information about reusing water and reducing water consumption. She also finds interesting information about dams, with terrific diagrams and statistics, but she knows that including that information will dilute her focus, confuse her readers, and take attention away from her main idea.

Transfer Your Learning

Across the Strands

Reading: As a reader, what advice would you give a writer to help make his or her ideas clear?

Across the Curriculum

History: What questions might you ask to narrow the topic for a paper about the development of Western Canada?

Talk About It

Do you believe that you can make a difference?

Kids Encouraged to Build Peace

Kosovo teen tells students around the world:
"You can still … make a difference"

Newspaper Article by Dale Anne Freed from the *Toronto Star*, December 10, 2007

Fatmire with Rudy Scholaert

With Kosovo poised to declare independence, Fatmire Feka, a teen from the war-torn Serbian province, brings her message of peace to an Ontario high school.

"Never give up on your dreams," Fatmire, a displaced Albanian Muslim, will tell the Grade 9 class at Vaughan Secondary School later today. Even if you're just a kid, "you can still make a change, still make a difference, no matter how small. By respecting your rights and others' rights you can build peace."

Fatmire, who calls herself "a refugee of the world," has brought her message to youth around the world, from Switzerland to Spain, Finland to Romania to Nairobi, and now for the first time to Canada.

Fatmire knows first-hand about staying positive. When Fatmire was 11, the civil war hit. She and her family fled to the mountains. Her sister, Sadet, 19, and her brother, Sami, 17, went missing. They have never been found. Fatmire saw skies that became empty of birds, grass that turned brown, cities reduced to rubble.

Developing Ideas ➔

The idea in writing is the main message or the story you're trying to tell. What is this reporter's main message or the story she is trying to tell?

Developing Ideas ➔

Narrowing the topic to something manageable is important. This reporter focuses on the narrow topic of a young woman's efforts to bring peace to Kosovo. The reporter tells that story without including a lot of detail about the war or Serbia.

Developing Ideas ⬊

If you're writing a story, stick with the major events. If you're writing nonfiction, focus on one idea and include a few supporting or interesting details. Notice how this newspaper article is like a story—it recounts the major events.

Developing Ideas →

Know your topic well enough that your ideas are strong and sound. What research did this reporter have to do?

Developing Ideas →

Don't include information that isn't essential to the main message. Notice how this reporter gives you very little background information. She expects the average reader of the newspaper to know something about Serbia and its war.

"But … I just couldn't give up," she said. "This is what my (missing) brother and sister wanted to see: Kosovo in a peaceful place."

When she was 12, Fatmire organized Kids for Peace, a movement to bring children from Kosovo's ethnic groups together. At a World Vision training centre in southern Kosovo, she read a poem and implored the adults present, "Will you help me make peace in Kosovo?"

At that time, she met Rudy Scholaert—a former World Vision "peace builder" stationed in Kosovo. He encouraged her to study hard and said he would sponsor her to university. "He brought me hope," she said.

With Rudy's help she started organizing peace-building workshops for four Albanian and four Serbian groups. By 2003, Fatmire was asked to join the city of Mitrovica's Council for Peace and Tolerance.

Fatmire and her sister, Zelihe, 17, have now made a home in Mississauga, where they hope to attend university. Fatmire wants to study international relations at the University of Toronto. This is all thanks to sponsorship from Rudy.

Fatmire, who came to Canada in August of 2007, now does volunteer work with World Vision Canada, training kids in peace-building. "This was my dream, doing the peace-building, working on peace-building. In the end it became a reality."

Background Information

In early 2008, a few months after this article was published, Kosovo gained its independence from Serbia, a country in the Balkan Peninsula. In the 1990s, the Kosovo Liberation Army fought against Serbian forces to establish its independence from Serbia. Many were killed, displaced from their homes, or forced to flee across the border as refugees.

Reflecting

Reading Like a Writer: Do you find that this article has a narrow enough focus for the reader to understand the topic? What suggestions for improving the article would you give this author?

Metacognition: What do you find challenging about developing your ideas for writing?

Making Connections: What personal experience would you draw on if you were writing a newspaper article about a global issue?

Talk About It
What do you already know about the issue of child labour?

What Is Child Labour?

Magazine Article by Chivy Sok

About 246 million children between the ages of 5 and 17 are engaged in child labour, according to the International Labor Organization's (ILO) global estimate from the year 2000. An estimated 73 million of these children are below the age of 10.

What is meant by *child labour*? What kind of work constitutes child labour? And where are these child labourers found? How is child labour connected to us? These are very simple questions. The answers, unfortunately, are not so simple.

It has taken many years to come to some kind of agreement on the definition of child labour. While experts continue to disagree on some aspects of the definition, two international human rights conventions have helped to guide international efforts to eliminate child labour.

The first comes from the 1989 UN Convention on the Rights of the Child. According to Article 32 of this convention, "**State Parties** recognize the right of the child to be protected from **economic exploitation** and from performing any work that is likely to be hazardous or to interfere with the child's education, or to be harmful to the child's health or physical, mental, spiritual, moral, or social development."

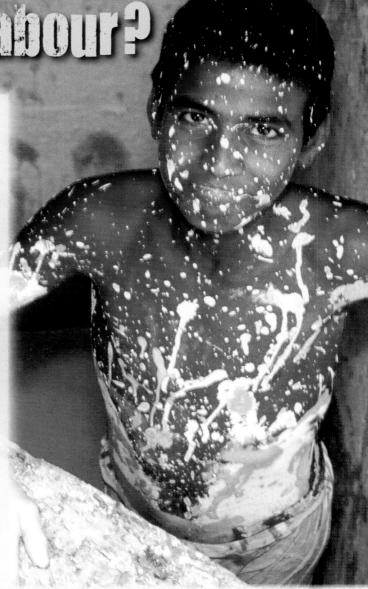

If you have ever made a clay pot, you know it's messy work. You might do it for fun—this boy does it to survive.

Vocabulary

economic exploitation: being taken advantage of in the production, distribution, or transfer of wealth, for example, being used as slave labour or forced to work in poor conditions

state parties: those countries that have formally approved and consented to a contract or agreement

A decade later, the ILO adopted a new convention that further defines the worst forms of child labour, the kind of work that is completely unacceptable and needs to be eliminated as soon as possible. The new ILO convention, commonly referred to as the Worst Forms of Child Labour Convention, defines the worst forms this way:

1. all forms of slavery or practices similar to slavery, such as the sale and trafficking of children, **debt bondage** and **serfdom**, and forced or compulsory labour, including forced or compulsory recruitment of children for use in armed conflict

2. the use, **procuring**, or offering of a child for prostitution, for the production of pornography, or for pornographic performances

3. the use, procuring, or offering of a child for illicit activities, in particular for the production and trafficking of drugs as defined in the relevant international treaties; and

4. work which, by its nature or the circumstances in which it is carried out, is likely to harm the health, safety, or morals of children. This last category is commonly referred to as *hazardous work*.

In 2000, the ILO conducted a study of the scope and magnitude of child labour. The Asia-Pacific region has the highest incidence of child labour. About 127.3 million working children between the ages of 5 and 14 are found in Asia, 73 million in sub-Saharan Africa, and 17.4 million in Latin America and the Caribbean. And about 5 million are found in developed countries and another 5 million in **transition economies**. This is only an estimate; it is nearly impossible to accurately measure the problem. But we know that this problem is widespread.

This 1998 Global March Against Child Labour was in Pakistan, where millions of children work to help their families survive.

Vocabulary

debt bondage: a form of labour, usually against one's will, to pay back something owed; often children are forced to work as slaves to pay off a family debt incurred generations previously

procuring: obtaining

serfdom: a form of slavery or forced labour in return for protection; a serf (a labourer) doesn't earn anything but the right to work the land and some of the food grown on the land

transition economies: countries in which the production, distribution, and transfer of wealth was controlled by the government, but now there is a free market and the prices of goods and services are determined by buyers and sellers

He's only 14, but he already looks like he's been labouring a long time. His work is crushing rocks to build a road, and he earns less than $1 for a 12-hour workday.
▼

Who picked the cotton that made your jeans? Children in Peru spend hours every day picking cotton, a backbreaking and thorny job.
▼

Not only are children working rather than going to school, but it is not uncommon in Africa to find children doing dangerous work, such as welding.
▼

When people hear the phrase *child labour*, they often think of problems in faraway places—problems in poor, developing countries. While it is true that the highest incidence of child labour takes place in these poor countries, North America also has this problem. In fact, North American history is filled with abusive forms of child labour, such as children working in mines, sawmills, and sweatshop factories. Today, some child labour continues to exist. We can still find children working on farms under some of the most hazardous conditions.

We are also connected to global child labour, directly and indirectly. About 70 percent of child labour takes place in agriculture. This includes the harvesting of bananas in Central America and cocoa beans for chocolate in West Africa and the picking of coffee beans and tea leaves in Latin America and Africa. Some of these agricultural products end up on our supermarket shelves. For better or for worse, we are connected to some of the most unacceptable forms of child labour.

Besides agriculture, what other forms of child labour exist? The list is long, and we can only cite a few categories to give an idea of the scope of the problem. Some children are

trafficked for forced labour or put into some of the most degrading kinds of work. Some are used to promote illicit activities such as the drug trade. Some children are kidnapped and forced to become child soldiers. Others are abducted to perform labour similar to slavery, such as becoming camel jockeys or working as servants in other people's homes. Other children, especially those orphaned by HIV/AIDS, are left to fend for themselves on the streets. These are the children who labour from dawn until dusk in dangerous conditions and live without knowing where their next meal will come from.

These 246 million children suffer from some of the cruellest human rights violations on a daily basis.

Chivy Sok is a human rights advocate.

Reflecting

Reading Like a Writer: What evidence did you find in this selection that the author carefully researched the topic?

Metacognition: How did making connections help you understand this article?

Critical Literacy: What did the author do to help you understand the reality of child labour?

Talk About It
What global issues are worth dying for?

CHILD SLAVERY PROTESTER

Nonfiction Article by Shirlee P. Newman

After being freed from a carpet factory, Iqbal Masih dedicated the rest of his short life to helping other children.

Ten-year-old Iqbal Masih lived in Pakistan. When he was four years old, Iqbal went to work in a hot, dusty carpet factory to pay back money his father had borrowed from the factory's owner. Iqbal could never pay it back. The owner charged him for his daily bowl of rice and fined him whenever he fell asleep as he worked. He'd have to work at the factory for the rest of his life, he thought.

Iqbal went to the police and told them how badly he was treated. The police listened to what he said, and then took him back to the factory. The owner beat him and chained him to the loom, the frame used to weave carpets.

MURDERED

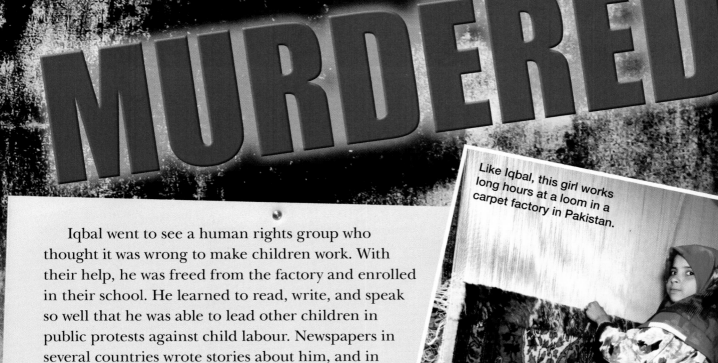

Like Iqbal, this girl works long hours at a loom in a carpet factory in Pakistan.

Iqbal went to see a human rights group who thought it was wrong to make children work. With their help, he was freed from the factory and enrolled in their school. He learned to read, write, and speak so well that he was able to lead other children in public protests against child labour. Newspapers in several countries wrote stories about him, and in 1994 he was invited to speak in Sweden and the United States.

For his efforts to end child slavery, Iqbal won the Reebok Youth in Action Award in December 1994. He planned to use the prize money for law school. He wanted to become a lawyer, so he could help to free other children, but he never got the chance. In 1995, Iqbal was shot and killed in Pakistan while he was riding his bicycle. Most people blame the carpet manufacturers for his murder because they lost business as a result of Iqbal's protest work. In 2000, the Sweden-based organization, Children's World, named Iqbal the winner of the first Children's Prize for Outstanding Children.

Reflecting

Reading Like a Writer: What is the main idea of this selection?

Metacognition: What connections did you make while reading? How did your connections help you understand Iqbal's struggle?

Critical Literacy: How might this article be different if it were told by the people who owned the carpet factory?

How to

Listen Effectively

Effective listening needs your active involvement—it won't just happen! To be an active listener, use the following strategies.

Strategy	Sample Text	You Might ...
Make connections between what you are hearing and your personal experiences or your knowledge of the topic.	Your geography teacher is talking about population distribution.	Connect this to a news item about how people in your area are moving away to find jobs in other provinces.
Visualize the information.	A speech by a politician states that 15% of Canadian children live in poverty.	Picture a school gym filled with 100 Grade 8 students—15 of those kids could be living in poverty.
Ask relevant questions of the speaker or yourself to keep yourself focused.	A radio report talks about a movement to buy local produce.	You might ask yourself: "What does she mean by buying local produce? Why is that important?"

Experiment with using different strategies as you listen to different types of texts on different topics. You might find that making connections works really well for you when listening to your friends tell a story, and questioning works really well when you're listening to your science or history teacher.

Transfer Your Learning

Across the Strands

Media Literacy: How can using these strategies for effective listening help you when you are watching the news?

Across the Curriculum

Science and Technology: Which of these strategies would you most likely use when listening to someone you don't agree with talk about global warming?

Talk About It

What sacrifices would you be willing to make to help someone in another country?

Lucille Teasdale

Transcript from Histor!ca Minutes

Uganda 1962

Listening Effectively →

One way to listen effectively is to make connections. What connections can you make to the first scene?

Opening scene: Uganda, countryside, under a tree sits a woman holding a baby. Pipe music reflects setting. Birds whistle, laughter, shouts of joy in background.

Text on screen: Uganda 1962

LUCILLE *(whispering to daughter)*: My angel. I'll love you forever and ever and ever.

VOICE-OVER: This is me and my mother, Lucille Teasdale.

Cut to: Lucille striding through small village. Sound of laughter, music, talking.

VOICE-OVER: One of Canada's first female surgeons. She came here with my Italian father to a medical mission in Africa.

Cut to: Suddenly there is screaming, chaotic scenes of war and dissolve to scenes of doctors tending patients, to ambulance, to village scene.

VOICE-OVER: Despite 20 years of civil war, together they built a modern, 500-bed hospital.

Cut to: Hospital room with Lucille tending young boy.

LUCILLE: Do you have a mother?

Sound effects: Shooting, screams

Cut to: Patients being rushed into hospital, doctors rushing around, Lucille running outside to help others.

Cut to: Scene in operating room, where Lucille is operating and cuts the palm of her hand; the patient's blood goes through her glove, infecting her; camera pans over nurse and doctors.

LUCILLE: Ow!

Predicting →

Visualize as you listen. What do you picture with the words *a modern, 500-bed hospital*?

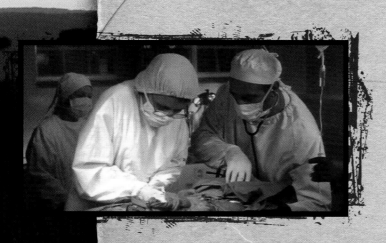

OTHER DOCTOR: Disinfect yourself!

LUCILLE: No, no time. This man's bleeding to death. I'll take antibiotics later.

Cut to: Lucille removing glove and putting new one on. She returns to operating on man. Dissolve to outside scene with tree, people, building in distance.

← **Listening Effectively**

Ask questions of yourself or the speaker. Would you delay disinfecting the cut? What does this decision tell you about Lucille Teasdale?

Text on screen: A part of our heritage.

VOICE-OVER: She performed the last of her 13 000 operations not long before she died ... of AIDS ... in 1996.

Text on screen: Lucille Teasdale 1929–1996.

Reflecting

Listening Effectively: What connections did you make to this selection? What visualizations helped you understand the selection?

Metacognition: If you're listening to a text that includes images, do the images help you understand what you're hearing? How might your answer to this question change the way you learn new information?

Text-to-World Connections: What world issues does this Histor!ca Minute highlight?

Talk About It

Do we own the world or are we simply its caretakers?

Who Owns

Oral Tale retold by Dan Yashinsky

One day a man who owned a field left it in the care of another man. He took good care of the land, ploughing, weeding, planting, harvesting it. When the owner came back he said to the man who had been taking care of it, "Give it back now. The land belongs to me."

"No," said the other man, "I won't. The land belongs to me. You are the owner, but I am the one who has taken care of the land all this time. The land is mine."

They went to find a judge to settle their dispute, and they came to Hodja. Each man said, "The land is mine, the land belongs to me!"

Hodja walked to the field, lay down in the dirt, and put his ear to the ground. "What are you doing, Hodja?" they asked.

the Land?

"I'm listening."

"What are you listening to?"

"The land."

Both men laughed. "Listening to the land? So what does the land say?"

Hodja looked up and said, "The land says that both of you belong to the land."

About Hodja

Hodja Nasrudin is a wise—though often considered foolish—folk hero. He's said to have lived during the Middle Ages somewhere in the Middle East. Many tales tell of how he solved differences and passed judgment with his curious outlook.

Reflecting

Metacognition: When you don't understand or agree with others, what effective listening strategies have you used to resolve any problems?

Text-to-Text Connections: When we watch movies or TV programs in which there is a dispute, we often see lengthy court cases. How is the resolution different in this selection? What has the storyteller done to create this difference?

Critical Thinking: Who do you agree with in this dispute: the man who tended the land, the man who owned it, or Hodja? Support your response with evidence from the text or your own experience.

How to **Recognize Purpose and Audience**

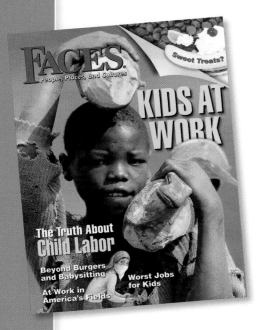

Producing media texts is very expensive. It's important to think about why these texts were produced and who they were produced for.

Purpose

All media texts are produced with a specific purpose. Some media texts, like weather or news programs, may want to inform you. Other media texts, like TV shows such as *Hockey Night in Canada*, may want to entertain you. Advertising is meant to sell you a product or convince you to think in a certain way. Knowing what the media creators want helps you to make judgments about the text.

Audience

All media texts are targeted to specific audiences. They are carefully *constructed* to appeal to certain people. For example, advertisers selling electronic equipment to young people will often stress the "cool factor."

Sometimes advertisers will create different ads for the same product. The individual ads can be targeted at different demographic groups. A cereal company might create an ad aimed at children aged 6 to 10 that emphasizes flavour and the prize contained in the box. Another ad for the same cereal might be targeted at parents and focus on nutritional content.

Knowing whether you are the target of a media text is important in helping you understand and respond to it.

Advertisers use the word *demographic* to describe the qualities of the audience they are trying to reach. A demographic group is a group of people who share measurable qualities. For example, an advertiser selling a new video game might decide to target the demographic group of young men aged 14 to 18 living in households where the annual income is over $45 000.

To determine and analyze the purpose and audience of a media text ask yourself:

- What is the primary purpose of this media text: to persuade, inform, entertain, or sell?

- What elements in the media text help me identify its purpose?

- Could the media text have more than one purpose? What are the secondary purposes?

- How effectively does the media text achieve its purposes?

- What is the source of the media text? Does that source—such as a specialty TV channel—give me clues about the audience?

- What specific audience would most likely find the language or images appealing?

- What demographic group is the media text targeting?

- How effectively do the elements in the text (such as actors, words, photos, colours, graphics, and music) appeal to this group?

When you're analyzing the purpose and audience of a media text, also consider what the creators of the media text *didn't* want to do or whom they *didn't* want to target. For example, it's important to remember that when you're looking at an ad for sneakers, its purpose is to sell, not inform. That same ad may appeal to you, but not your parents, by using images or text that your parents won't appreciate.

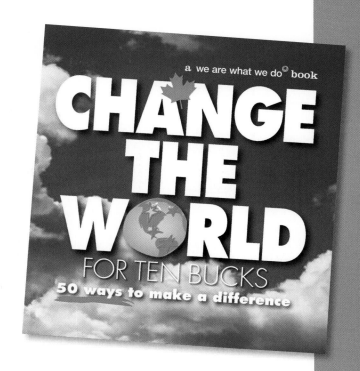

Transfer Your Learning

Across the Strands

Writing: What is the most important thing you have learned about recognizing purpose and audience that can help you connect to your readers?

Across the Curriculum

The Arts: How can you use your knowledge of purpose and audience to analyze the illustrations in a picture book?

Talk About It

In your opinion, what makes an ad effective?

SELLING CHANGE

Magazine Ads from various sources

Recognizing Purpose and Audience →

All media texts are created with a clear purpose. Is this ad intended to provide you with information, persuade you to a certain action, sell you something, or entertain you? What elements in the ad helped you identify its purpose?

Recognizing Purpose and Audience →

All media texts are created for a specific audience. How does the use of language or images help you to determine the intended audience for this ad?

Change your world

Over 150 volunteer projects worldwide rely on GVI. **So can you**

30+ countries including wildlife conservation in South Africa, Kenya, the Amazon & Costa Rica

GLOBAL VISION INTERNATIONAL

Volunteer overseas on critical humanitarian and conservation projects

info@gviusa.com

888-653-6028 (toll free)

VOLUNTEER—YOUR PASSPORT TO ADVENTURE

GL❂BAL VOLUNTEERS

Give us three months of your life and we'll give you a lifetime of adventure, experience, and learning.

We need young Canadian volunteers for projects overseas. Choose where you'll help: in schools, hospitals, or wildlife areas, with over 50 locations to choose from in Europe, Asia, South America, and Africa. We'll help you find the right volunteer project and get you where you want to go.

Call 1-800-555-9530

YOUTH CHALLENGE INTERNATIONAL

Make a world of difference

YCI involves Canadian youth in hands-on projects in developing countries:

Africa, the Americas and the South Pacific

If you are:
• Aged 18 to 30
• Interested in seeing the world
• Seeking a team based experience
• Available for 5 to 12 weeks

SUMMER PROGRAMS NOW AVAILABLE!

← **Recognizing Purpose and Audience**

Recognizing the purpose and audience of a media text can help you respond to it and judge its effectiveness. How effective is this ad? What makes it effective or not effective?

← **Recognizing Purpose and Audience**

Think about what the media text *doesn't* do. What purpose *doesn't* it have? Who isn't targeted? Why is it important to ask those questions about this ad?

Reflecting

Media Literacy: Which ad do you find most effective? Why do you think it's effective?

Metacognition: How does identifying the purpose and audience of an ad help you better understand its meaning?

Critical Literacy: All the ads from the original sources for this selection featured female volunteers. Why do you think that is? How do you respond to that choice? How might others respond?

Talk About It

How much money would you guess the average family spends on food each week?

Global Kitchens

Photo Essay by Peter Menzel and Faith D'Aluisio
from *Hungry Planet: What the World Eats*

Today we are witnessing the greatest change in global diets since the invention of agriculture. Globalization, mass tourism, and giant *agribusinesses* (large corporations running agricultural businesses) have filled our supermarket shelves with extraordinary new foods.

This photo essay reveals what people eat during the course of one week. Each family's photo includes a portrait of the entire family at home surrounded by a week's worth of groceries.

The extended Ahmed family has 12 members. They live in the same apartment building in Cairo, Egypt, and eat many of their meals together. Food for one week is approximately $70.

Namgay and Nalim's family has 13 members. They live in Shingkhey, Bhutan, a remote hillside village of a dozen homes. Food for one week is approximately $5. The market value of their home-grown foods, if purchased locally, would be approximately $30.

The Casales family has 5 members. They live in Cuernavaca, Mexico. Food for one week is approximately $190.

The Manzo family has 5 members. They live in Palermo, Italy. Food for one week is approximately $260.

The Patkar family has 4 members. They live in Ujjain, India. Food for one week is approximately $40.

The Brown family has 7 members. They live in Riverview, Australia. Food for one week is approximately $376.

Reflecting

Media Literacy: What do you think is the purpose of this photo essay? What audience do you think would be most interested in the original book, *Hungry Planet: What the World Eats*?

Metacognition: What do you learn from this selection about the presentation of information that you might use elsewhere?

Critical Literacy: The original source for these photos did not feature a Canadian family or photos. What do you think a typical Canadian photo would include? In your opinion, what photo here most closely reflects a Canadian family?

Sequence

The following samples show the beginning of an outline. Each entry can be filled in with more detail.

Events in Time Order

1. First, I met my host family.

2. Next, we went out to the tree-planting site.

3. Then, I was introduced to the international team working at the site.

Most Interesting Events First

1. I met over 20 people from 6 different countries.

2. By my last day, I had planted over 400 seedlings.

3. Every night, we had a terrific party, teaching each other new dance steps.

You're excited about the trip you took to Brazil. You want to share all your experiences with your classmates. You could list everything that happened from when you got off the plane to when you got back on. You could tell about the most exciting events first, followed by less exciting events. Both methods use sequence text pattern.

Recipes, science experiments, and instructions are examples of sequence text pattern. The pattern writers choose will depend on their purpose as well as the topic. Sequence text pattern is used when the purpose is to list something (events, instructions) in a certain order.

When you recognize the pattern, you will find it easier to understand the purpose of the text and how ideas are connected. Look for these characteristics of sequence text pattern:

1. There is an order to how things are listed and the order is important.

2. Events or instructions may be arranged in numbered steps (or using the letters of the alphabet).

3. Lists (sometimes with bullets) may be used.

4. Keywords may be used (for example, *first, soon, initially, now, before, gradually, meanwhile, later, next, today, once,* or *soon after*).

Transfer Your Learning

Across the Strands

Oral Communication: Would you be more likely to use sequence text pattern for a speech about a volunteer experience you have had or for an oral presentation on global warming? Be prepared to discuss your thinking.

Across the Curriculum

Health: If you were developing instructions for washing hands, how many steps would you need? What major steps would you include?

Doctors Without Borders

**Diary by staff from
Doctors Without Borders**

*Since its beginning in 1971, Doctors Without Borders has helped
countless people. Do you wonder how the organization knows
where to send volunteers and how many to send? The following
diary entries show how the organization went into action when
large numbers of Sudanese refugees began pouring into eastern
Chad in September 2003.*

Sequence Text Pattern ➔

In sequence text pattern,
there is an order to how
things are listed and the order
is important. How does the
structure of this selection
clearly indicate the order
of events? How does this
selection indicate that the
order is important?

Day 1: Assessing the Needs

Doctors Without Borders sent an exploratory team to
determine the condition of Sudanese refugees flooding into
eastern Chad. The people were fleeing conflict and targeted
attacks against them in the Darfur region of Sudan.

The team found about 11 000 refugees, 75 percent of whom
were women and children, living in harsh conditions with little
or no access to food, *potable* (drinkable) water, or shelter. They
found no local supplies of medicine, and surveys indicated
that there was a significant risk of an outbreak of measles or
meningitis because very few of the refugees had been vaccinated.
Many of the children suffered from malaria and malnutrition.

Doctors Without Borders Operating around the World

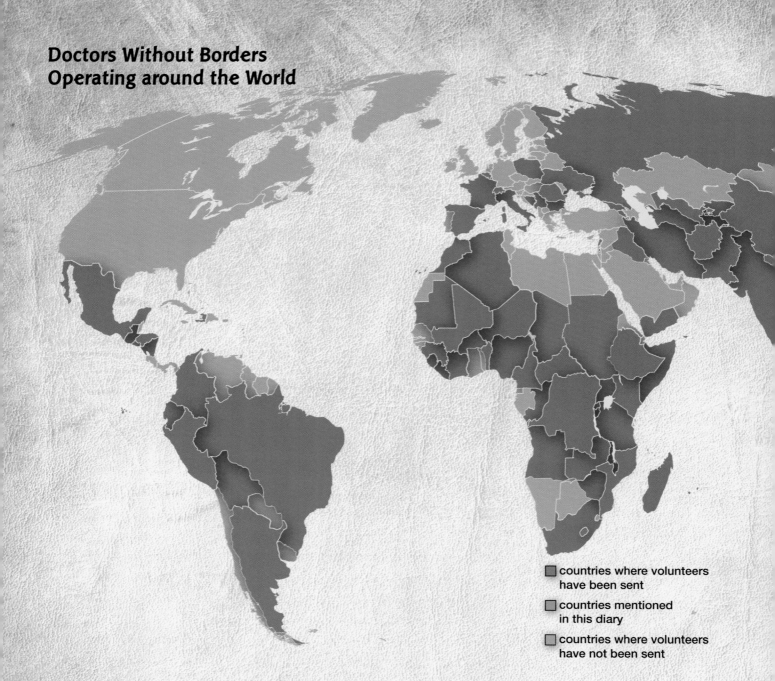

- ■ countries where volunteers have been sent
- ■ countries mentioned in this diary
- ■ countries where volunteers have not been sent

Day 5: Planning the Response

The assessment team started treating patients immediately, and reported back to the Doctors Without Borders team in the capital city of N'Djamena. The health priorities of the refugees had to be addressed quickly in order to save lives. An emergency intervention, including vaccinating all children for measles, providing essential health care, increasing the supply of potable water, and planning for the treatment of malnutrition, was implemented. An 11-person team, including doctors, nurses, and **logisticians**, was sent within days to carry out the aid operations.

Doctors Without Borders through Time

← Sequence Text Pattern

Your purpose for writing can influence the pattern you choose. Certain formats and features are associated with sequence text pattern. Notice that this selection uses both diary entries and a timeline; both are good choices when you want to list a series of events in order.

1971 A group of French doctors and journalists creates Doctors Without Borders in reponse to famine in Nigeria

1972 Responds to its first natural disaster, an earthquake in Nicaragua

1975 Provides medical care in its first large-scale intervention to help Cambodian refugees

1976 First major intervention in a war zone: Lebanon

1980 Programs offer medical care to civilians during Soviet Union's invasion of Afghanistan

1984 Starts programs to fight malnutrition in response to famine in Ethiopia

1986 Organizes mobile clinics and hospitals to aid victims of civil war in Sri Lanka; opens offices in Spain and Luxembourg

1990 Opens office in United States

1991 Runs largest emergency operation to date, providing care for Kurdish refugees in Turkey, Iran, and Jordan

1992 Informs international community of famine in Somalia; opens nutritional programs there

1993 Provides aid to victims of civil war in Burundi

1994 Issues unprecedented call for military intervention amidst **genocide** in Rwanda

1995 Brings medical aid to civilians in Chechnya and nearby refugee camps

1996 Launches massive vaccination and treatment program to combat meningitis epidemic in Nigeria

1997 Expands programs to help children in Madagascar, Brazil, and the Philippines

1998 Fights to help women in Afghanistan get health care

1998 Responds to famine in southern Sudan and civil war in Republic of Congo; assists victims of Hurricane Mitch in Honduras, Nicaragua, Guatemala, and El Salvador

1999 Launches Campaign for Access to Essential Medicines; provides care in Kosovo, Albania, Macedonia, Montenegro, and Serbia

1999 Awarded Nobel Peace Prize

2000 Treats victims of civil war in Sierra Leone; expands programs for **asylum seekers** and **undocumented immigrants** in France, Italy, Spain, and Belgium

2001 Starts providing medicine to people with AIDS in 7 countries; expands mental health programs

Vocabulary

asylum seeker: a person who flees his or her home to gain shelter or protection in another country

genocide: the deliberate, systematic killing of a whole cultural or racial group

logistician: an expert in the coordination of a complex operation including many people and things

undocumented immigrant: a person who illegally enters a country other than the country of his or her birth

Day 12: Dispatch of Team and Supplies

A chartered cargo plane left from the Doctors Without Borders warehouse carrying 33 t of humanitarian aid and the 11 international volunteers. The cargo contained material to build two health centres, medicine and supplies to treat 10 000 people, feeding kits, and specialized food for malnourished children for a period of three months. The plane also carried three four-wheel drive vehicles and equipment to provide clean water, including pumps, pipes, tanks, and water-purification chemicals.

The plane arrived the same day in N'Djamena. The cargo was unloaded and put on another plane to the closest town, and then it was driven seven hours over very rough terrain to the refugee camp.

Day 20+: Building Health Centres

Doctors Without Borders opened its first health centres in Tine and, four days later, a therapeutic feeding centre for severely malnourished children was built. Four tents were set up to provide medical care for thousands of refugees living in camps outside the town. The tents housed a consultation room, pediatric unit, pharmacy, and in-patient areas.

2002 Runs largest operation to date to aid famine victims in Angola

2002 Arjan Erkel, member of Doctors Without Borders, is abducted in North Caucasus

2003 Provides care during U.S. invasion of Iraq and to victims of fighting in Liberia and Democratic Republic of Congo

2003 Becomes a partner in new organization to develop medicines for neglected diseases; raises over $50 million

2004 Runs feeding centres, clinics, and vaccination campaigns in Sudan

2005 Treats 63 000 malnourished children in Niger with a new ready-to-use-therapeutic food (RUTF); provides care to people caught in the violence in Haiti's capital

2006 Sets up surgical program in Jordan to care for war-wounded patients sent from Iraq; returns to Sri Lanka to provide care for people fleeing war in the north

2007 Campaigns against companies blocking access to essential medicines; aid worker, Elsa Serfass, is killed in Central African Republic; calls for international humanitarian response in Chad as violence displaces 150 000 people

Reflecting

Analyzing Text Patterns: If you wanted to arrange the timeline not chronologically but by most important events, which three events would you place first? Which three events would you place last?

Metacognition: How does knowing about sequence text pattern help you understand the selection's purpose?

Critical Literacy: What words in this selection clearly reveal the author's perspective on Doctors Without Borders?

Talk About It
What does art have to do with global issues?

Art, Politics, and Questioning Authority

Autobiography by Ilona Dougherty

What do you want to be when you grow up? Alive. I carried this slogan around on my protest sign at an anti-nukes march. It was my first protest. I was three years old. My family always encouraged me to challenge ideas in the world around me. When I was in Kindergarten, my mom sent me to school with a T-shirt that boldly commanded, *Question Authority*. At the same time, my parents worked hard to make sure my brother and I understood that it was important to contribute to our global community.

By 14, I was a self-declared **activist**. I was always the odd one out in junior high: while other kids watched TV after school, I planned conferences and protests. There was always something to be done. I learned the ins and outs of the activist community. On the flip side, I discovered a sense of community with a group of people who were passionate about making positive change in the world.

In Grade 12, I started to evaluate the function of the activist community. What was effective about our work? And how could we be more effective? I began to question what really inspired me.

APATHY IS BORING
L'APATHIE C'EST PLATE

In my hometown of Whitehorse, for our upcoming graduation I organized a school talent show. At the event, one of the acts was a punk band called SOL whose energy and drive captured my imagination. Working with SOL offered a different, more creative way to reach people. I started working with them, and we produced a CD and booked shows.

The skills I'd learned as an activist translated easily into working with artists. But the two worlds were so different—these musicians could get kids out to shows; it wasn't a struggle to get people to show up and to listen. The five guys in the band brought loud music and the constant sense that something was about to happen.

I'd found a creativity that the activist community lacked. I saw just how much music could affect people and make them feel strongly about something. Getting this kind of enthusiasm was something my fellow activists weren't that good at. They could talk to politicians and reach out to people who already cared, but they couldn't seem to reach youth who didn't already know about the issues. I realized that art could speak to that audience. If we could blend the **accessibility** and emotional hook of art with the passion and conviction of my activist colleagues, then I felt that positive things would start happening—that we could both inspire and activate.

After high school, I set this theory into motion. I auditioned for a contemporary dance program at Concordia University in Montréal. The year after I finished my degree at Concordia, I co-founded **Apathy** is Boring. Based in Montréal, Apathy is Boring uses art, media, and technology to engage youth in the democratic process. This project allows me to draw on both my artistic and activist sides every day.

Youth in Canada don't trust politicians, only 36 percent of us went out to vote in the 2006 election, and the number of youth who volunteer in their communities keeps shrinking. Apathy is Boring works with musicians, celebrities, and political parties to create forums that break down the barriers between youth and political leaders. We're breaking the rules about who has access to people with power.

Vocabulary

accessibility: the condition of being easily understood, appreciated, or approached

activist: a person who takes action in promoting his or her views or aims on a social or political issue

apathy: a lack of interest in or desire for something; indifference

The formula is simple: put young people somewhere they feel comfortable—like a concert or online—bring politicians there, and see what happens.

At a concert we held in February 2005, we brought together Euphrates, an Iraqi hip-hop emcee, a Conservative member of Parliament, and a Green Party representative. It could have been a recipe for disaster, but the respect they offered one another when they shared the stage was amazing. The event really represented what Apathy is Boring is trying to accomplish.

Apathy is Boring challenges institutions like the Canadian government and the United Nations to really listen to what young people have to say. I work through Apathy is Boring to consult with the government on how to become more youth-friendly. At the same time, we reach out to young people to show them where they have the opportunity to be heard.

So far our work has been well received. Over our first two years, we've been able to reach about 500 000 young people. We've run two successful "get out the vote" campaigns during federal elections, which included a public service announcement that ran in major movie theatres across the country for a week, media appearances on every channel from MuchMusic to CBC Newsworld, and a website that showcased quotes from musicians alongside resources like a voting how-to guide.

Every day I re-evaluate the work I do as we explore new ways of engaging young people. I ponder how far we can take the art before our message becomes too abstract.

As Apathy is Boring continues to build momentum, we keep working to find ways to turn our democratic traditions into living traditions that will change and adapt to facilitate wider participation. I appreciate the grandness of that challenge. I'm glad the slogan I carried when I was three years old has been fulfilled: my spirit is totally alive, inspired, and passionate about making positive change in my community happen in artistic and unpredictable ways.

Reflecting

Analyzing Text Patterns: Develop a graphic organizer that shows the main events in this sequence text.

Critical Literacy: In your opinion, is this selection fair to everyone? Who might object to some of Ilona's points? Use evidence from the text and your own experience to support your answer.

Geography

The reading strategy you learned in this unit can help you to better understand text in other subject areas. Make connections as you read this geography text. Use those connections to draw conclusions.

Where People Live: Population Distribution

Population growth is the primary source of environmental damage.

– Jacques Cousteau,
oceanographer and environmentalist

Fact File

Eighty percent of the world's people live in countries that are economically developing, and 97 percent of all population growth occurs in these countries. The United Nations uses the term *economically developing* to refer to countries that are not as industrialized as Canada or the United States; these countries are mainly in Africa, Asia (except Japan), and Latin America.

For thousands of years in human history, Earth was home to relatively few people. At the end of the last Ice Age—about 10 000 years ago—there were somewhere near 10 million people worldwide. It wasn't until about 1950 that the population started to grow quickly. In the 1990s, the world's population grew by around 80 million people a year. Official estimates by the United Nations predict that by the year 2050 the world's population will have grown to around 9 billion people, and that it will continue to grow over the next two centuries.

In 1999, the world's population reached 6 billion—a huge number to grasp. How many years would it take to count to 6 billion at a rate of one number per second? (Hint: There are 86 400 s in a 24-h day.)

Counting Heads

Demography is the study of human population. Demographers are scientists who study data on population and issues related to where—and how well—people live. Geographers and demographers try to help us understand why people live where they do and why some countries have population problems. As part of their work, demographers help countries, regions, and cities predict what the population will be in the future. They are hired by governments and businesses to make recommendations about how to provide services and goods for people.

The Census

How are all the people in a country counted? Every five years, governments collect information about the number of people living in their region. Every 10 years, a more detailed census is carried out: people are hired to conduct door-to-door surveys in their neighbourhoods, collecting information about age, ethnic background, language, family size, and other facts. Statistics Canada is the branch of government responsible for the Canadian census.

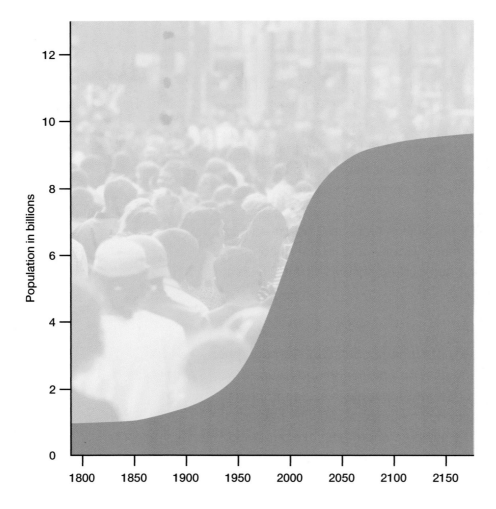

World population growth, 1800 to 2150 (estimated). What do demographers mean when they say there has been a population "explosion"?

Reflecting

Making Connections: What connections did you make as you read this text? What conclusions did you draw as a result of those connections?

Metacognition: How did making connections as you read help you understand this text? What other strategies from the unit helped you?

TECH THEN AND NOW

How have changes in technology impacted our world?

Unit Learning Goals

- question text to increase understanding
- organize ideas in writing
- deliver oral presentations
- ask questions to evaluate media texts
- analyze narrative text pattern

Transfer Your Learning: Mathematics

How to # Ask Questions

Asking questions before, during, and after reading can help you to make sense and clarify your understanding of a text. There are three kinds of questions you can ask about a text:

- **_Literal_ or "On the Line" Questions:** The answer is directly stated; it's found on the page in one or several places throughout the text. For example, ask yourself, "What does the text say explicitly about the main character?"

- **_Inferential_ or "Between the Lines" Questions:** These are questions where you have to connect clues or information in the text to something you already know in order to get an answer. Think about what the author implies as well as what is stated directly. Sometimes you'll find the answer to an inferential question later in the text. For example, ask yourself, "What can I infer about the main character from what he/she says or does or what others say?"

- **_Evaluative_ or "Beyond the Lines" Questions:** These are questions about the text's quality, logic, or perspective. Your answers to these questions judge the text, using evidence from the text and your own ideas. You must go beyond the text by thinking deeply about it and responding appropriately.

While it's important to ask questions of a text, it's also important to think about your answers, and whether there might be other answers to those same questions. Especially with evaluative questions, other readers may respond differently than you have.

Sample Evaluative Questions

- Does the text reflect sound research or reasonable thinking?

- How does this text compare with others that explore the same issue?

- Does the author have an obvious point of view or bias? Do I agree with that viewpoint?

- Whose voices are missing from this text and how does that affect the telling?

- What opinion do I form about this text? What justifies that opinion?

Transfer Your Learning

Across the Strands
Media Literacy: What questions do you ask to help you evaluate a movie review?

Across the Curriculum
Mathematics: Evaluative questions can be asked when you are double-checking someone else's work. Which of the above questions would you use when you are evaluating another student's solution to a math problem?

Talk About It

What do you already know about the types of products produced from recycled material?

Paving from Plastic

Young Gina Gallant Brings New Life to Garbage
Profile by Sandra Phinney

Asking Questions →

As you read, ask literal questions. Answers to literal questions can be found in one or several places in the text. Ask yourself, "How old was Gina Gallant at the time Sandra Phinney wrote this profile?"

Asking Questions →

As you read, ask inferential questions. Use clues in the text and what you already know to answer the questions. Ask yourself, "Why didn't the engineers believe in Gina?"

Three years ago, while driving with her family in Cache Creek, British Columbia (locally referred to as "Trash Creek" because of a massive landfill site nearby), Gina Gallant suddenly thought, "Wouldn't it be great if we could use garbage to pave roads?" She was 13 years old at the time.

After doing some research to learn about how asphalt is made, and conducting some basic experiments on grinding up plastics such as pop bottles and milk cartons, Gina met with city engineers in her hometown of Prince George, British Columbia. She was proposing a new kind of pavement that would use plastic waste.

"One of [the engineers] didn't believe that this was my idea and the other said it was too big a project for such a young person," she recalls. Gina didn't take it as an insult. Instead, she turned it into a challenge and went on to prove she could.

First, she learned that 33 percent of British Columbia's landfill sites are made up of discarded plastics: that's a lot of milk jugs and pop bottles. Recycling plastics to pave roads would reduce garbage and reduce the use of natural resources for asphalt.

Gina knew that the first rule of inventing is "Don't reinvent the wheel," so she researched earlier efforts to build roads out of waste materials. She came across many trials using glass and rubber, but glass isn't compatible with asphalt. She couldn't find any examples where recycled plastics were being used. She reasoned that since plastic and asphalt are both petroleum-based materials, the two substances should be compatible, and her idea should work.

First, Gina went to Husky Oil, which was established in Prince George to produce a variety of petroleum products and heavy fuel oil. They were also bringing in large quantities of asphalt from their head office in Calgary. Gina had prepared herself ahead of time and went to great lengths to explain what she intended to do and how her idea could benefit the community. Her enthusiasm and presentation convinced them she was serious about the project, and the officials at Husky Oil let her use their lab to do some experimenting.

Over 100 experiments and many weeks later, she found the winning combination: 6 percent plastic, 6 percent asphalt, and 88 percent crushed rock. She then used a machine to compress the mixture into pellets—and finally had a product called PolyAggreRoad (PAR). It just needed a bit more testing and fine-tuning before she could take it to market.

Unfortunately, the city engineers wanted more proof. "I had to get companies on board to do more pellet testing with the same blends and mixes that the city of Prince George was using," Gina explains. When the city makes a blend, they use Mix C aggregate (a mixture of four different types of rock) and asphalt. Before determining if they could ever use her pavement on a road, she had to test her blend using the city's Mix C aggregate to ensure that her pavement would work using their standards.

Gina Gallant is shown here in the lab at work on her paving material.

It didn't take long for Gina to rally support. Husky Oil provided asphalt and aggregate; Ingenia Polymers of Calgary provided recycled plastic powder; AMEC Earth and Environmental tested PAR; and Columbia Bitulithic said they would build a patch of test road for her. The companies all agreed to participate for free to support Gina's endeavours.

In October of 2003, with the backing of the four companies, the mayor of Prince George gave Gina the green light. She was able to oversee the paving of an L-shaped piece of road 49 m long by 3.7 m wide on Cranbrook Hill Road.

Time will tell how her pavement stands up to the wear and tear of vehicles and the natural elements, but there are early indications from engineers that PAR will be more durable than regular roads.

Down the road, Gina hopes that her product will be accepted for industrial use and mass produced. "I'd like to see [PAR] reducing garbage in landfills all over the world," she says. Meanwhile, Gina intends to keep inventing.

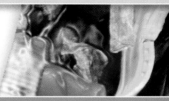

← Asking Questions

As you read, ask evaluative questions to form opinions. Ask yourself, "What did these companies gain by supporting Gina's invention? How might environmental activists feel about this plastic paving? Could there be any drawbacks to this invention?"

← Asking Questions

As you read, ask evaluative questions to understand the author's point of view. Ask yourself, "What is this author's opinion of Gina? What is my own opinion about Gina and her invention?"

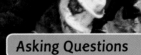

Asking Questions

A graphic organizer like this one can help you to organize your questions.

Literal Questions	Inferential Questions	Evaluative Questions

Reflecting

Questioning: What questions did you ask as you read this profile? Were you able to answer all your questions?

Metacognition: Which question allowed you to gain a deeper understanding of the selection? What does that tell you about the types of questions you should ask as you read other texts?

Critical Thinking: What is the message this author is trying to send? How do you respond to that message?

Talk About It
What would you consider the greatest invention in the toy or game world?

Rubber Shortage Leads to Silly Putty

Nonfiction Article by Don Wulffson

In 1942, during World War II, the United States experienced a shortage of natural rubber (natural rubber comes from the rubber tree plant). A synthetic, or artificial, form of rubber was needed for the production of gas masks, boots, and tires. The military turned to the General Electric Company for an answer.

At the company's lab in New Haven, Connecticut, James Wright tried every chemical combination he could think of. Nothing worked. Then he mixed boric acid with silicone oil. The mixture formed a soft, rubbery compound.

Excited, James began experimenting. He discovered that when tossed on the floor, the plastic putty didn't just bounce—it bounced better and higher than rubber. It also stretched farther, didn't decay, wouldn't crack in extreme cold, and wouldn't melt in extreme heat.

Almost anything could be done with it—except the one thing it was supposed to do: serve as a substitute for natural rubber. It simply didn't get hard enough.

Years passed, the war ended, and the fascinating flop was all but forgotten. Until, one evening in 1948, an engineer from General Electric went to a party. Coming straight from work, he happened to have a glob of Bouncing Putty with him. For laughs, he started showing others at the party some of the fascinating things it could do. Everyone thought it was interesting. A woman named Ruth Fallgatter thought it was more than interesting: it was a toy!

Not surprisingly, Ruth Fallgatter was a toy store owner. Accompanying her at the party was Peter Hodgson, a friend who helped her write sales and advertising material for her store.

A few days later, Peter and Ruth met to put together her holiday catalogue. After talking it over, they decided to include Bouncing Putty on a page spotlighting gifts for adults. Their ad read, "Do a thousand nutty things with Bouncing Putty. Comes in a handy clear plastic case. A guaranteed hoot at parties! Price: Only $2.00!"

Surprisingly, Bouncing Putty sold better than almost everything else in the catalogue. Ruth continued stocking the product in her store, but she had no interest in manufacturing and marketing it. Peter Hodgson did. He made an agreement with General Electric to buy Bouncing Putty from them. He hired students from Yale University to separate the putty into 28-g balls and package it in plastic eggs. Because *bouncing* described only one of the many different things the substance could do, Hodgson changed the name to something catchier—*Silly Putty*.

A few months later a writer for *The New Yorker* magazine bought some Silly Putty in Manhattan. He was so excited by its strange properties that he took it to work with him the next day and wrote about it. Incredibly, within three days, orders for Silly Putty had topped a quarter of a million dollars. Peter Hodgson became a success story.

Silly Putty was soon available all over North America. The substance that had bombed so badly for the military bounced back as a bestselling toy.

Reflecting

Questioning: Which of the evaluative questions listed on page 58 did you ask of this selection? What answer would you give that question?

Metacognition: How did asking evaluative questions increase your interest in this article?

Critical Thinking: How does your understanding of toys and their appeal help you to understand the success of Silly Putty? How important do you think the right name is to a product's success?

Talk About It
What are the characteristics of a great inventor?

Light Bulb

Concrete Poem by Joan Bransfield Graham

Thomas
Edison didn't
hesitate to let
ideas incubate, and
try again, if they
weren't right. One
day to his intense
delight, he squeezed
his thoughts
into a bulb
and then
turned
on the
light
light
light
!!!

My Fluorescent Flow

Poem by Michelle Muir

I may be compact
And fairly new on the scene,
But I'm lighting up the world in ways
Thomas Edison had only begun to dream
In the innumerable machines in his mind.
My light shines and intertwines
And twists, and turns, and burns
With an energy-saving glow
And just so you know,
I'm leaner, and greener, and cleaner
Than ever before.
Mr. Edison would've been pleased
With what we've achieved
With the idea he conceived
I wonder if he knew
That what he imparted
Helped get us started
On the road to invent
Tubes of glass
That contain a gas
That glows when electric current
Passes through it.
I wonder if he knew it
Was gonna be
An idea with a bright future.

Reflecting

Questioning: Asking questions can help you compare texts on similar topics. What is similar about how Edison and his creation are described in these poems? In your opinion, how important are both these inventions?

Metacognition: How does comparing the poems affect your response to each poem?

Critical Thinking: What techniques did the poets use to influence your response?

Talk About It

"Everyone starts out as a scientist, asking questions and exploring the world around them."

INSPIRED TO INVENT

Rachel Zimmerman Invents the Blissymbol Printer

Profile by Maxine Trottier

On a cloudless night in mid-August 1980, Rachel Zimmerman gazed up at the sky with a sense of wonder. Her parents, Linda and Walter, had driven Rachel and her younger brother, Gary, into the countryside, far from the bright lights of their home on St. James Street in London, Ontario. There, as they did each summer, the family watched the Perseid meteor shower. This year, though, it was more special to Rachel than ever.

She had always liked science, but just months before, Rachel's teacher, Anne Lane, had taught her about the planets in the solar system. Her class went on a field trip to the observatory at the University of Western Ontario in London. Looking through a telescope for the first time, Rachel began a relationship with outer space and inventing.

Rachel didn't consider herself to be an inventor in the beginning. A good student, she entered the science fair at St. George's Public School each year with projects including "The Constellation Orion." One of her home inventions had a very practical side. "I invented something I called the *Great Cake Grate*, which was used to make sure every slice of cake was the same size," she recalls. "This solved the problem of arguing with my brother over who got the biggest piece of cake for dessert."

During Grade 6, 11-year-old Rachel began working on an invention that would end up being useful for people everywhere. She had started reading books about people with physical challenges, and the work of Charles Bliss gave her the idea for her next science fair project. Charles Bliss had invented a universal language called Blissymbolics. In 1972, the year Rachel was born, it was being used enthusiastically by a young teacher at a treatment centre in Toronto, now called Bloorview Kids Rehab. The language is a system of symbols that can be used by people who have cerebral palsy, who sometimes can neither speak nor control their hand movements well. Wanting to share what she had learned, Rachel did that year's project on Blissymbolics.

Charles Bliss's system of communicating by pointing to symbols was good, but not perfect. By Grade 7, Rachel was working on a computer-controlled device that would let people use Blissymbolics to write messages independently. Her mother, Linda, had a computer software development company. She taught Rachel how to program her computer. Both of her parents greatly encouraged her. So did her Grade 7 teacher, Bill White, with his "Go for it!" attitude.

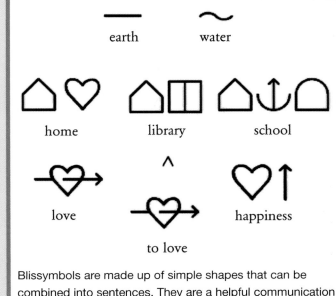

Blissymbols are made up of simple shapes that can be combined into sentences. They are a helpful communication tool for non-speakers.

Rachel created an overlay (a paper representation of the symbols to show users where to press for each symbol) with 100 Blissymbols and four control keys: new message, backspace, English/French, and print. The overlay was mounted on a touch-sensitive board that plugged into a computer. She then wrote a computer program to make the computer "recognize" the board's symbols. When the user touched a symbol, the computer translated it into a word. Sentences could be seen on the monitor and "typed" on a printer.

Rachel's project placed first in her school science fair, and then won the London and District Science and Technology Fair. The next month, Rachel and her project won a silver medal and an IBM award at the Canada-Wide Science Fair. At 13, Rachel Zimmerman was invited to represent Canada with her project at the World Exhibition of Achievements of Young Inventors in Plovdiv, Bulgaria. She can still remember trying to find Bulgaria on a globe.

Rachel displays her project at the World Exhibition of Achievements of Young Inventors in Plovdiv, Bulgaria, 1985.

Rachel tested the printer with Bliss user Kari Harrington. Kari shared a poem she had written about how she wanted people to see her for who she was inside and not to judge her by her cerebral palsy. Kari now edits a website for Bliss users.

Rachel Zimmerman went on to London Central Secondary School, then to Brandeis University in the United States and the International Space University in France. She has worked for the Canadian Space Agency, NASA, and other space organizations. Today she is an education and outreach coordinator at Caltech in California, a job that combines her love of science and her commitment to young people and learning.

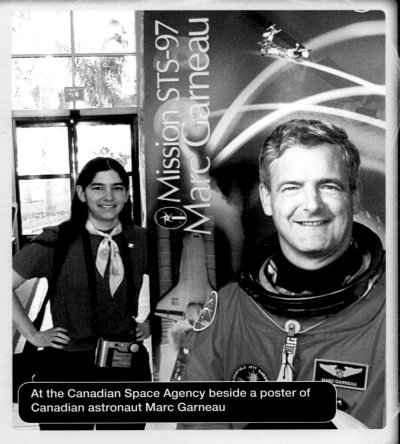

At the Canadian Space Agency beside a poster of Canadian astronaut Marc Garneau

"Science and engineering are very important to Canada's future," she has said. "Everyone starts out as a scientist, asking questions and exploring the world around them. This natural curiosity can lead to exciting discoveries and new inventions. Never lose your sense of wonder about the world."

Look where that sense of wonder has taken Rachel Zimmerman.

Reflecting

Questioning: What questions did you ask yourself that helped you make inferences or evaluate the text?

Metacognition: Think about the types of questions you asked yourself. What types of questions did you ask most often? What does this tell you about how you think about texts?

Critical Thinking: Think about the results and implications of Rachel's invention. How could inventors use new technology to improve on Rachel's invention?

How to ➤ Organize Ideas

When you write informational text, an organizational pattern makes your writing more fluent and easier for your readers to understand.

Organizational Pattern	What It Means
Sequence	Steps or events are told in order.
Problem/Solution	A problem is presented and one or more solutions suggested.
Compare and Contrast	Similarities and differences between two topics are described.
Description	The characteristics or attributes of a topic are described.
Generalization	A general statement is made and supported.

Check that your text is organized logically by looking for the following:

1. The pattern makes sense for your topic and purpose for writing. For example, if you want to explain the steps in a science experiment, you would use sequence text pattern.

2. Your main idea has prime importance and is usually first stated in the opening paragraph. You refer back to your main idea elsewhere in the text, especially in the conclusion.

3. You lead readers from one idea to the next by using transitions or keywords. For example, *however*, *nonetheless*, *since*, *because*, *in conclusion*, *as a result*, and so on.

4. Your headings help readers follow the text. You may also use visuals, lists, charts, or graphic organizers in your text to help your readers understand your ideas.

Transfer Your Learning

Across the Strands

Oral Communication: When giving a presentation, you need to make your organization of ideas even more apparent than when someone is reading your work. Which of the above tips do you think would be especially helpful when you are speaking?

Across the Curriculum

Science and Technology: Science makes frequent use of cause-and-effect, sequence, and problem/solution text patterns. Why are these common patterns in science texts?

Talk About It

What do you predict the world will be like when you are 50 years old?

FUTURE VISIONS
Yesterday versus Today

Nonfiction Article by Valerie Wyatt

Organizing Ideas ↑

The pattern makes sense for the topic and purpose for writing. From the title, what pattern do you predict this writer will use?

Organizing Ideas →

The main idea is usually first stated in the first paragraph. What is the main idea of this selection? How does that idea reflect the organizational pattern?

Their Tomorrow

Your own personal helicopter. Food in the form of pills. A robot to make your bed. These were some of the far-out predictions people made about the future 50 years ago. These days, we see the future in a vastly different way. How did those predictions go so wrong?

People imagine the future based on what is around them today. Fifty years ago, air travel was becoming popular. Why not more of it, in the form of two-person planes and helicopters? Fast foods, canned or frozen, were speeding up meal preparation. Popping a food pill was the logical next step. As for the bed-making robot ... robots were all over the movies. It seemed inevitable that they would roll into the home.

Personal Robots? Not Yet! Online Shopping? Yes!

Here are some *accurate* predictions people made 50 years ago:

- stoves that cook food in seconds—we call them microwave ovens

- fast transmission of documents—through e-mail and fax machines

- TVs that allow you to shop without leaving the house—online shopping

Our Today

Organizing Ideas →

Transition words help the reader to follow your thinking. What text patterns (besides sequence text pattern) might use these transition words?

Back then, technology was seen as the route to a brighter tomorrow, and new machines played a big part in people's view of the future. Today, on the other hand, we live with the effects of technology. Some of these effects are good—we live longer thanks to medical advances. But others, such as pollution caused by the boom in airplane travel and too many vehicles, have put us on the path to climate change.

Our Tomorrow

Organizing Ideas →

Writers sometimes use headings to help their readers. How do the headings help you understand this article?

Our ideas of the future are more cautious about technology than our great-grandparents' were. We see the dark side as well as the bright. Like them, we base our projections on what we see around us today. They saw personal aircraft because the skies were empty. We imagine renewable fuel cars because the roads are packed with pollution-spewing vehicles. While they saw food pills, we see nutraceuticals (noo-trah-SOO-tuh-kuls). Nutraceuticals are foods genetically engineered to protect us from disease.

As for that robot? Fifty years from now, robots may not only be making beds but also removing your appendix, driving your car, and playing soccer with you. Not only that—they will be smart. In fact, their artificial intelligence may make them smarter than humans.

Nanotechnology may also change our world. It is the technology not of wood and steel but of molecules. The result may lead to super small things, such as microscopic trucks that carry atoms and molecules around in miniature factories, and super strange things, such as clothes that clean themselves or change colour.

Our future predictions have something in common with those of our great-grandparents in that they are based on the familiar. But what about those bad guesses they made (food pills) and wild cards (climate change)? They remind us that making predictions can be, well … unpredictable. What will the future be like? Only time will tell.

Reflecting

Reading Like a Writer: How do the headings support the organizational structure chosen by this writer?

Metacognition: What process do you use to analyze text patterns? For example, do you scan the text looking for transition words that give you clues about the pattern?

Media Literacy: How has the media influenced your thinking about the future?

Talk About It
"An apple a day keeps the doctor away." How true do you think that old saying is?

Road Dust and Writing

Nonfiction Article by Richard Platt from *Would You Believe ... Cobwebs Stop Wounds Bleeding?*

The story of real cures and healing began some 4000 years ago in the Middle East. The Mesopotamian people, in the land that is now Iraq, were the first to have real doctors. They still cared for their patients with a mixture of magic and medicine, but they had learned to wash and dress wounds, and operated using sharp copper knives.

To speed healing, Mesopotamian doctors used drugs, some of which had no healing effect at all. Medicines included pills made from lizard dung, but most were plants. Doctors used more than 230 plants, including fig, sesame, laurel, and apple.

The cure for a blow to the cheek was a mouthwash made from the dust of four crossroads.

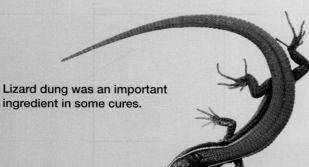

Lizard dung was an important ingredient in some cures.

King's Code: Much of what we know about Mesopotamian medicine comes from the Code of Hammurabi. This was a list of laws made by King Hammurabi of Babylon sometime before 1750 BCE. The laws were carved on a tall stone, which wasn't found until 1901 CE. Some of the text on the stone says what doctors can and cannot do, and gives the punishments for those who break the law.

Scientists and Sorcerers

Mesopotamia had two types of doctor—the *ashipu* and the *asu*. The *asu* prescribed herbal cures, while the *ashipu* was a spiritual healer and prescribed charms and spells to drive out the demon or god believed to have caused the disease.

The best Mesopotamian doctors grew rich from their skills. A major operation cost as much as a house. The price of failure was high, too. Surgeons who botched an operation would have a hand cut off.

Dressing Up

The Mesopotamians were the first people to use plasters, or dressings, to treat wounds. They made a paste using ingredients such as plant resin and animal fat, smeared this paste on the wound, and kept it in place with a bandage. The paste helped to keep the wound clean and prevent infection.

Studying how doctors healed in Mesopotamia teaches us about more than how medicine began; it also gives us a fascinating insight into the culture of the civilization.

Healing Hound: The sitting dog was a symbol of healing in Mesopotamia. It took on special meaning 4300 years ago when rabies, a disease spread by dog bites, struck the land.

 Treatments included dressing wounds with mud from the river.

Reflecting

Reading Like a Writer: This article uses descriptive text pattern. How does its pattern match its purpose?

Metacognition: How do the visuals and captions support your reading of this selection?

Critical Literacy: What is the author's point of view in this article? What evidence from the article supports your answer?

Talk About It
What do you think a "nano doctor" is?

NANO DOCTORS ON CALL

Informational Report by Sandy MacPherson

One morning you struggle out of bed so dizzy you can hardly walk. Your muscles ache, your head hurts. It's time to see the doctor.

Your doctor takes one look at you and says, "Swallow this." She hands you a small pink pill. The pill, she tells you, contains a tiny computer that will monitor the cells in your body and send back data that she'll use to diagnose your condition.

Broken bones rebuilt with nanotechnology will heal faster than they do today.

If this sounds like science fiction, well, it is. But it may not be for long. Thanks to a new kind of medicine based on *nanotechnology* (the science of the super-small), computers tiny enough to fit in a pill are just one of the marvels that are likely to be common in the next few years and decades.

Welcome to a Nanoworld

Today, when you break a bone, you can look forward to weeks in an awkward, often itchy cast. But in the future, new nanomaterials, such as nanotubes, which look like tubes of chicken wire, only smaller than a human hair, may provide a strong scaffold for new bone growth and cut recovery time drastically. Nanomaterials may one day also be used to improve skin, build stronger muscles, and even create artificial organs, such as kidneys.

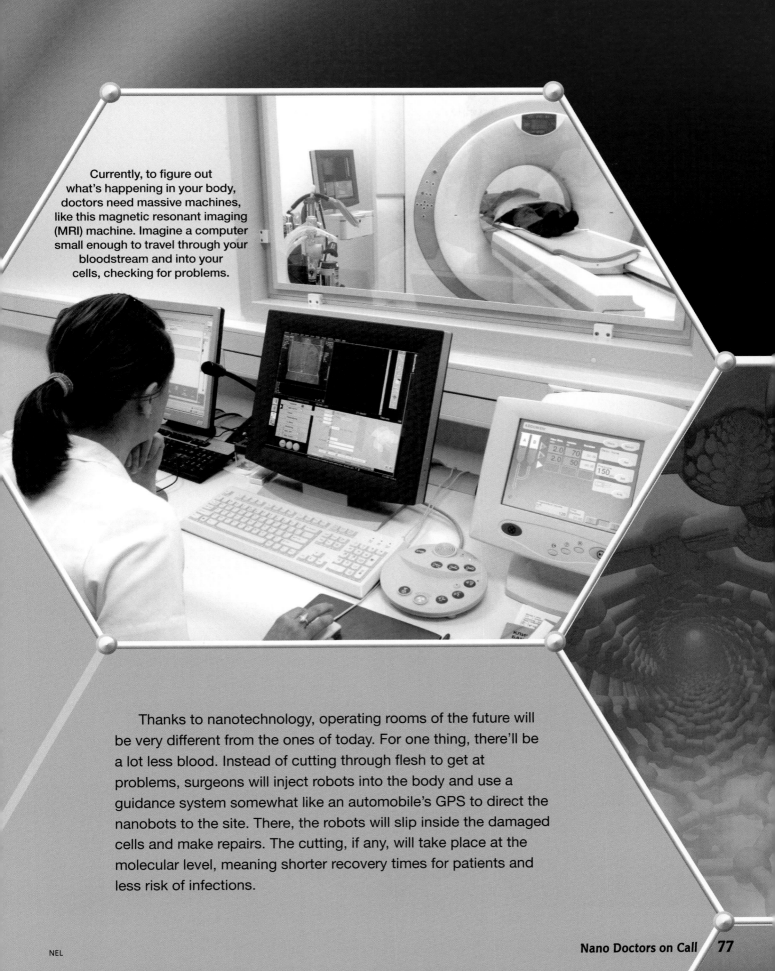

Currently, to figure out what's happening in your body, doctors need massive machines, like this magnetic resonant imaging (MRI) machine. Imagine a computer small enough to travel through your bloodstream and into your cells, checking for problems.

Thanks to nanotechnology, operating rooms of the future will be very different from the ones of today. For one thing, there'll be a lot less blood. Instead of cutting through flesh to get at problems, surgeons will inject robots into the body and use a guidance system somewhat like an automobile's GPS to direct the nanobots to the site. There, the robots will slip inside the damaged cells and make repairs. The cutting, if any, will take place at the molecular level, meaning shorter recovery times for patients and less risk of infections.

Nanobots will also revolutionize drug treatment. At present, for example, people with cancer are often treated with harsh chemicals that kill healthy cells as well as cancerous ones. This chemotherapy can make patients sick. But in the future, nanobots (tiny robots) with cancer sensors will hunt down and deliver drugs only to cancer cells. This precise targeting of cancer cells will mean fewer side effects for patients and better cure rates.

Nanomedicine to the Rescue?

We've known for a long time that diseases happen in the cells of our bodies or in the molecules that make up the cells. Nanotechnology will, for the first time, allow doctors to get inside the damaged cells to repair or remove them. And, because nanomachines and materials are so small, there is less risk of rejection by the body. They can even be engineered to look like the body's own molecules. Amazingly, compared with other medical innovations, nanotechnology is cheap. Materials such as nanotubes and machines such as nanobots can be assembled from ordinary molecules that are available everywhere.

Forget about the side effects of drugs—you won't get any. Nanotechnology will send tiny drug-carrying robots directly to damaged cells to deliver just the right amount of drugs to repair or eradicate those cells.

Surgery as we know it may become a thing of the past as tiny robotic surgeons do repair work inside your cells instead.

Some people warn that nanotechnology has potential for harm as well as for good. If nanomaterials can make muscles stronger, will soldiers and athletes equipped with them have an unfair advantage? If nanoprobes can locate individual damaged cells, will they find so many that everyone will be considered sick? And what happens with all the information that nanoprobes gather about people? Is there a way to keep the data secure, or will people's privacy be violated?

Despite these concerns, scientists believe that nanomedicine is worth pursuing because it has the potential to make people healthier. While not all of the technologies you've read about here will materialize, they are not just science fiction. Nanotechnology is already being used in other parts of society. Some wrinkle- and stain-free clothes use nanotechnology, as do certain kinds of sunscreen and golf balls. Building on what we already know about nanotechnology, scientists are hoping for a bright future for nanomedicine, where diseases will be diagnosed early and cured.

Reflecting

Reading Like a Writer: What is the purpose of this selection? How is the selection organized effectively for its purpose?

Critical Literacy: Does this selection treat both sides of the topic fairly? Use evidence from the text to support your answer.

How to ▸ Deliver Presentations

Two people are given the same assignment. They research exactly the same information and both speak clearly. Yet one presentation just turns out okay, while the other one is GREAT! Great presentations come from a combination of important content and powerful delivery. Try these tips to help you give a great presentation.

1. Start your presentation in an engaging way; with a question, a startling fact, a personal story, or a vivid image. You want your audience to connect with your topic.

2. The language you use—whether formal or informal—is also a factor in engaging and connecting with your audience.

3. Make the organization of your thoughts clear. Tell your audience early on what your main message is, and then every point you make should build on the main message.

4. Have passion, energy, and conviction in your voice, which comes from really caring about and believing what you are saying.

Transfer Your Learning

Across the Strands

Writing: How could you use the tips above to help you improve your writing?

Across the Curriculum

History: If you were giving a presentation in history class about how technology has changed society, what personal story could you share to engage your listeners?

Talk About It
What answer do you give to the question in the title? Why?

Can Machines Learn?

Speech by Richard Young

Richard Young prepared this speech for an audience of high-school students.

Delivering Presentations →

Good speakers start their presentation in an engaging way. How does Richard Young help his audience connect to his topic?

Delivering Presentations →

Good speakers clearly identify their main message and then continue to emphasize or build on it. What is Richard's message? How does he build on it?

For most humans, walking and talking come easy. Just a few years after we're born, we're *aces* at both. We can even do them at the same time—while chewing gum!—and we don't have to think about it. But robots, with their *fancy* computer brains, can't walk or talk much better than toddlers, despite 50 years of trying.

What's the deal? How come a "smart" machine that *eats* math calculations for breakfast starts spouting gibberish if you ask it a simple question about trees or clouds?

Computers can do some things *extremely* quickly and accurately, such as storing and retrieving *enormous* amounts of data, multiplying *huge* numbers together, and delivering e-mail messages around the world. But computers are *terrible* at other things. A truly intelligent machine that can talk with humans or cross a room without bumping into things is *still* the stuff of science fiction.

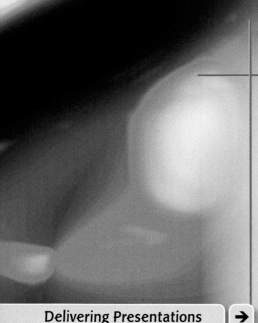

Delivering Presentations →

The language you use is also a factor in engaging and connecting with your audience. What language does Richard use to engage his audience?

There's a lot of disagreement about the definition of intelligence, but most people would agree, for example, that a **log** does *not* have it. **Frogs**, on the other hand, do. They can make decisions based on what they see and hear around them: they can hop away from danger, and they can hunt and catch flies. Dogs are smarter still: not only can they remember things and react to their surroundings, but they can also communicate with people by barking, yelping, face licking, and tail wagging. Moreover, they can learn. A dog can be taught tricks, and it learns plenty of things without being taught.

So, where do computers fall on our Log-Frog-Dog Smart-O-Meter? Somewhere between logs and frogs. Surprised you all, didn't I? That's right, a computer that can play **chess** is still NOT as smart as a **frog**!

It's true that in 1997 the IBM computer Deep Blue defeated chess master Garry Kasparov. It's also true that playing chess is *easier* than walking, talking, or catching flies. In chess, each piece can move only a couple of different ways, and at each point in the game only certain moves are possible. Because Deep Blue was so *amazingly* fast **(400 million positions calculated every second!)**, it could "think" several moves ahead and then choose its best move.

The REAL world, however, is not like chess. A day in the life of a frog may seem simple, but the number of things that can happen is ridiculously huge and, even worse, impossible to calculate. For starters, there are no simple rules for where the frog can and can't hop to next. It's the same thing with chatting or walking across a room. There are not enough simple rules to guide a robot, and the many different possibilities overwhelm it. These kinds of open-ended problems are a robot's worst nightmare.

But there's hope! We already know of a machine that can solve open-ended problems. You're using one right now: it's the human BRAIN. Scientists don't know exactly how it works, but they've managed to use some of what they do know to create a kind of simplified mini-brain called an Artificial Neural Network (ANN).

Some say that ANN is just another program running on just another computer. On the face of it, that's true. But *this* program is special—it can reprogram itself! An ANN can get information from the real world and then use it to improve itself. Over time, the ANN gets better at its task, just as if it were **learning**.

An interesting thing about these learning machines is that we can't always predict *what* they'll pick up on. In one funny example, scientists tried to teach an ANN to find army tanks in a forest. The ANN *appeared* to learn the difference between photos of forests with and without tanks. But, when it came time to look at new pictures, the ANN failed BADLY. After a lot of head scratching, someone realized that the pictures used to train the ANN had a strange quirk. All the pictures with tanks were taken on a sunny day, and all the pictures without tanks were taken on a cloudy day. So the ANN had actually learned to detect *shadows*, not tanks!

The human brain is one of the biggest mysteries in science. We've figured out just a bit about how it works, and that's been enough to help scientists build machines with some intelligence, including the capacity to learn. Not bad considering we've been at it for only a few decades while nature has had a 10-million-year head start! Perhaps, as we learn more about the brain and as computers get faster and more powerful, we'll be able to build machines that can learn completely on their own, or even from each other. Just like we do.

← **Delivering Presentations**

Good speakers are passionate about their topic. Where in this paragraph is Richard's passion for his subject obvious?

Reflecting

Communicating Effectively: Assess Richard Young's speech using the elements listed on page 80.

Metacognition: What did you learn from Richard's speech that you could use to give a speech of your own?

Critical Literacy: What is Richard's message? What is his bias? How do you respond to that message?

Talk About It
What do the Bionic Woman, Darth Vader, and Dr. Octopus have in common?

My Superheroes

Speech by Chris Bahar

Chris Bahar is a Grade 8 student. He was born with one arm missing and has a prosthetic arm—a myoelectric arm that moves in response to nervous signals sent to the muscles in his upper arm. He gave this speech to his class as he presented his science fair project on bionics.

The posters on my bedroom wall remind me I'm not alone. And I'm not the first. For centuries, humans have used technology to help make their bodies fitter, faster, or more flexible. It's a technology called bionics—using mechanical devices to replace parts of the body or help the body work better.

So on my wall, I have old posters of the Bionic Man and the Bionic Woman, Darth Vader, the Borg from *Star Trek*, and Dr. Octopus from *Spider-Man 2*. These heroes and villains are all part human, part machine.

The idea of bionic technology goes back centuries. Thor, a Norse god, had iron gloves that helped him lift and crush boulders and a belt that doubled his strength. There's a poem from India that's over 4000 years old that tells how Queen Vishpla lost one of her legs during a battle. She went back into battle wearing an iron leg.

The idea of bionic technology isn't just in myths, stories, movies, and TV shows. The first bionic arm was a myoelectric or electronic arm developed at the University of Utah in the 1970s. This arm uses tiny computer chips, sensors, batteries, and motors to turn nerve signals into movement in an artificial hand. The wearer can make fine movements, like turning a page or tapping the keys on a keyboard.

An arm like that can cost over $70 000! I've outgrown a couple of arms, since my first one. Luckily, there's actually a Myoelectric Limb Bank where you can exchange an old arm for a new one. Each arm, of course, has to be custom fitted for the person wearing it. As well, you can get hands designed for your hobbies or activities—baseball or bike riding or playing the drums.

The list keeps growing—of the parts of the human body that can be replaced or enhanced by a machine! Hearts, limbs, joints, eyes, ears. It's exciting to think about how far this technology has advanced in the last 40 years. And it's amazing to think about what the future may hold. This sort of technology may help humans live in hostile environments—on Earth or on other planets. Maybe tiny computer chips implanted into the human brain will help us remember things.

Until the future gets here, I'll keep on collecting stories of people who have that mechanical edge, and posters for my bedroom walls. Every time I look at them, I'll remember, I'm not alone, I'm not the first, and I won't be the last.

Thank you for listening.

Reflecting

Delivering Presentations: How effectively does Chris organize his speech?

Metacognition: What strategies does Chris use to help you understand the topic of bionics?

Critical Literacy: What is Chris's perspective on bionic technology? What questions did you ask yourself about this selection? What questions about bionic technology are not raised in this selection?

FOCUS ON MEDIA

How to ➤ Evaluate Media Texts

Behind every media text can be found a set of assumptions. For example, the publisher of a sports car magazine may assume that new cars should be faster and more powerful. On the other hand, the publisher of an environmental magazine may assume that all cars should have better fuel efficiency. These assumptions are based on the values these publishers hold.

All media texts are influenced by the values of their creators. In some cases the values behind a media text are obvious. The producer of a fashion show values style and beauty. The creator of a blog about alternative bands values her style of music.

In other cases the values of a media text are not obvious. If a TV series always presents athletes as being poor students, it implies successful students can't be athletes. If a commercial only shows wealthy people having fun with a product, the unspoken message is you need to be wealthy to be happy.

As consumers of media, it's important that we make choices about the media we consume based on our values, and not permit our values to be replaced or overwhelmed by someone else's values. We should always question the assumptions behind a media text. We must always consider not only what the media text is showing or telling us, but also what it's leaving out.

Questions to Consider

1. Do the characters look like people from my neighbourhood?

2. Is the situation presented in the media text realistic?

3. Do the characters in the text reflect my values?

4. Can I think of someone who would find this media text upsetting or offensive?

As you look at the comic strips on these pages, consider what the artists/creators value and whether anyone would find the text upsetting or offensive.

Zits comic strip, created by Jerry Scott and Jim Borgman

Sherman's Lagoon comic strip, created by Jim Toomey

Transfer Your Learning

Across the Strands

Writing: When you write a story, how do you convey to your readers what your characters value?

Across the Curriculum

Health: Think about a media text you've experienced recently that deals with a health issue. What assumptions were made by the creators of that text? What values are connected with those assumptions?

Talk About It

How long can you go without stepping outside? How long would you want to go?

FUTURE SCAPES

Posters from
Amazing Stories **and**
by Christopher Short

City of Their Future

In 1939, futuristic dreams often took the form of cities like the one shown here, which first appeared on the back cover of the sci-fi magazine *Amazing Stories*.

Evaluating Media Texts

Identify the assumptions the creator of the media text has made. What assumptions were made by the people who created this futuristic poster?

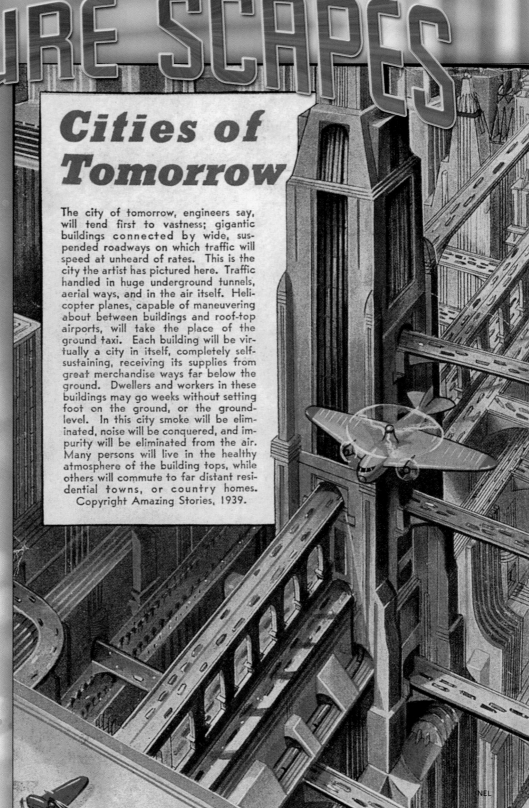

Cities of Tomorrow

The city of tomorrow, engineers say, will tend first to vastness; gigantic buildings connected by wide, suspended roadways on which traffic will speed at unheard of rates. This is the city the artist has pictured here. Traffic handled in huge underground tunnels, aerial ways, and in the air itself. Helicopter planes, capable of maneuvering about between buildings and roof-top airports, will take the place of the ground taxi. Each building will be virtually a city in itself, completely self-sustaining, receiving its supplies from great merchandise ways far below the ground. Dwellers and workers in these buildings may go weeks without setting foot on the ground, or the ground-level. In this city smoke will be eliminated, noise will be conquered, and impurity will be eliminated from the air. Many persons will live in the healthy atmosphere of the building tops, while others will commute to far distant residential towns, or country homes.
Copyright Amazing Stories, 1939.

Urban Environments of the Future

Welcome to your future! In the 21st century, scientists, engineers, and architects forecast a world where cities will accommodate the needs of both people and nature. In designing any living space, the priorities will be ecological and sustainable living as well as the needs of the individual.

City of Our Future

This poster was created in 2008 for this student book.

Evaluating Media Texts

Ask questions to analyze the values of the creator of the media text. What does the creator of this poster value? Who might not agree with those values?

Reflecting

Media Literacy: How do you respond to these posters? How does your emotional or personal response affect your evaluation?

Metacognition: What strategies helped you evaluate these posters? For example, questioning the texts' assumptions, comparing the images to other similar ones, or discussing the posters with your classmates.

Connecting to Other Media: What movies or TV shows present a view of the future similar to that presented in either poster? How does making that connection help you evaluate these posters?

Talk About It

A car that runs on grass! What possible disadvantages could it have?

"Grassoline"

Comic Strip by Tom LaBaff, the creator of Nestor's Dock

What is that and how can I get one?

It's my grass-powered car.

Excuse me?

Yeah, all I do is take a bunch of grass clippings and dump them in here. I call it the . . .

grass tank!

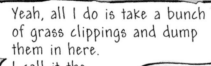

Then I just crank it up. Hop in.

Wow! This thing really works. Where to?

Detroit. I'm going to sell this design to Big Motors so they can start making cars that don't use gasoline.

Yeah, and stop polluting the air!

Reflecting

Media Literacy: What does the creator of this comic strip value? What evidence in the text supports your answer?

Metacognition: How do you respond to this comic strip? How does your response affect your evaluation?

Narrative

A straightforward narrative follows this pattern:

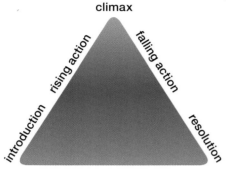

climax

rising action

falling action

introduction

resolution

This diagram shows a straightforward narrative. The diagrams for more complex narratives will vary, depending on whether the story is told in chronological order, or when a subplot is introduced or the subplot action begins.

1. **Introduction:** the writer introduces characters, setting, and problem or conflict.

2. **Rising Action:** a series of events develop the problem or conflict.

3. **Climax:** the character(s) succeed or fail at solving the problem.

4. **Falling Action:** the action falls rapidly after the highest point of tension, the story's climax.

5. **Resolution or Denouement:** falling action leads to the story's ending or conclusion.

Complex Narratives

One type of complex narrative is when the story is not told in chronological order. For example, the story begins with the main character's death and then explains how he or she died. Another type is when **subplots** are used. Subplots are additional plot lines that follow along with the main story. Subplots can help us understand the characters or setting. Subplots are usually resolved at the same time as the main story.

Transfer Your Learning

Across the Strands

Media Literacy: Movies often use complex narratives. What was the last movie with a complex narrative that you watched?

Across the Curriculum

History: If you were going to write a short story for history class about the experiences of a teenaged pioneer settling in Canada, what subplot might you include?

Talk About It
Do you ever think you have too many rules?

The Zarg Tyranny

Short Story by Valerie Thame

Narrative Text Pattern →

Introduction: The writer introduces the characters, setting, and problem or conflict. What is the source of conflict in this story?

"But why do we need all these rules?" demanded Jade.

Her mother's eyes narrowed. "You've been talking to Miriam again," she said. "Ignore her, Jade. Cratern cannot exist without Zarg rules."

"Well, you would say that," said Jade. "You're a lawyer."

"And you are fourteen years old," said her mother crisply. "You have a highly trained mind, but it is sadly flawed by your ridiculous curiosity—which you did not get from me."

"Who made these rules anyway?" said Jade. "And why can't they be changed? Some of them are so stupid. Why can't I call you mother? Why do we have to use PIN numbers all the time?"

Jade's mother looked horrified. "Watch your tongue," she hissed. "You know as well as I do that Zarg rule is not to be questioned. Just keep your opinions to yourself!"

L42 looked anxiously about the room. All accommodation units were bugged, and L42 was afraid that her daughter's rebellious remarks would be overheard and she would be to blame. The punishment for disobedience was severe, but L42 did not think it unjust. She saw nothing wrong with the Zarg system for all Craterns. She herself had been a model pupil. At eighteen she had qualified as an attorney and afterward had a brief relationship with a scientist known as S11—Jade's father.

Jade often thought about the father she had never seen. She wondered what he looked like, or if she was like him. Apart from her mother and Miriam, she knew nothing of her family. Craterns looked only to the future and Zarg law disapproved of looking back. Jade was fascinated by the past. She wanted to know who she was and where she came from.

Her grandmother, who shared the small accommodation unit, often spoke of the old times and of Jade's grandfather, Kern.

"He was a brave but foolish man," said Miriam, "and asked far too many questions. Much like you, Jade. The Placators came and took him away and I haven't heard from him since. Zargs are tyrants! Dictators! And I hate them all!"

Miriam fumbled under her bunk and pulled out a much treasured volume of paper bound in leather. "This is a history of the planet Earth," she said, carefully turning the fragile pages, "and I wouldn't be surprised if we originally came from there. Earth was populated with beings not unlike ourselves, Jade. They had longer legs because they walked a lot, but smaller heads because they only had little brains."

"Mother says Earth has never sustained life."

Miriam sighed. "It's no good talking to your mother. She sees things differently. She's told me that if I insist on speaking my mind she'll report me."

"She wouldn't!" protested Jade.

"Who can say, but let's not worry about that," said Miriam. "Let's see what we can find out about Earth, shall we?"

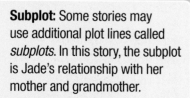

Narrative Text Pattern ➔

Subplot: Some stories may use additional plot lines called *subplots*. In this story, the subplot is Jade's relationship with her mother and grandmother.

Together they browsed through the forbidden book. Jade was fascinated by the idea that such a dull, dead planet could have ever been alive, with seas and trees and people. She had only seen computer graphics of other worlds and had no real concept of a sea, except that it was a vast expanse of water controlled by another planet called the Moon. She noticed some handwriting on the first page of the book.

"That," said Miriam proudly, "was written by my grandfather, your great-great-grandfather."

"*Vox et praeterea nihil*," read Jade. "It doesn't mean anything to me."

"Nor me," said Miriam. "But your great-great-grandfather was a clever man. He must have thought it important."

"It could be in code," said Jade. "We could work it out. I could access the main data banks. I think I know how."

"Good girl," said Miriam. "But be careful—and tell nobody. This shall be our secret."

Secret or not, the Zarg spy network picked up Miriam's whispered words and early the following morning the Placators came and took her away. They would not say why she had to go nor where she was going. Jade made inquiries via the Infonet but was told that information was not available. It was classified.

L42 carried on as if nothing had happened.

↙ **Narrative Text Pattern**

Subplot: Subplots can help you understand the characters or the setting. How does the subplot involving Jade, L42, and Miriam help you understand the setting?

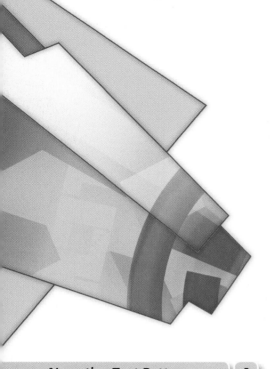

Narrative Text Pattern →

Rising Action: A series of events develop the problem or conflict. What important events have happened so far?

Jade knew there was little chance of ever seeing her grandmother again. The Zarg rule was callous and unjust. The Zargs were ruthless tyrants. The only clue to something better was those four curious words from the past. *Vox et praeterea nihil.* More than ever Jade wanted to find out what they meant.

So Jade spent part of the time in her Training Module trawling through forbidden directories and data banks looking for a clue to the history of Cratern and the beginning of Zarg rule.

She was able to work undetected because Training Modules had no tutors. The pupils received their instructions only through headsets, and any communication between pupils was strictly forbidden.

Jade had been trawling for nearly a month without success when she found archive material showing three-dimensional examples of ancient artefacts of Earth—strange and curious objects labelled *Hair Dryer, Candles, Bicycles, Tennis Racquets, Envelopes.*

She also found a bibliography with screen after screen of book titles. She found a thesaurus of language. Earth, it seemed, had almost as many languages as books—Urdu, French, Greek, Latin—but she could not decipher any of them. It was while she was looking at languages that her screen blanked out.

Jade tried to retrieve the program. The grim face of a Zarg appeared. The grey eyes locked onto hers, the mouth moved, but Jade could hear nothing. Then she remembered her headset was switched off.

"Fool, fool," she told herself angrily as she flicked the switch.

"The information you have accessed," intoned the Zarg through the headset, "is classified. Feed in your personal code and number and await confirmation of status."

The Zarg disappeared. Jade was well aware that if she keyed in her pupil number the Zarg would know she had no right to be looking at those old files. The Placators would come and take her away and that would be that.

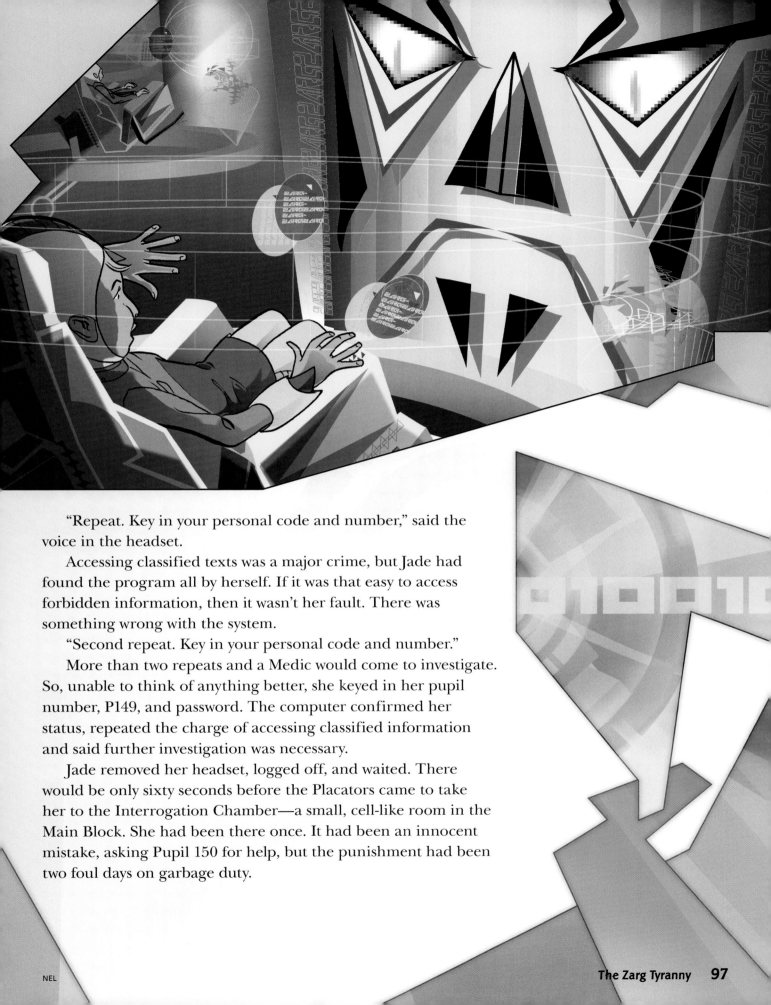

"Repeat. Key in your personal code and number," said the voice in the headset.

Accessing classified texts was a major crime, but Jade had found the program all by herself. If it was that easy to access forbidden information, then it wasn't her fault. There was something wrong with the system.

"Second repeat. Key in your personal code and number."

More than two repeats and a Medic would come to investigate. So, unable to think of anything better, she keyed in her pupil number, P149, and password. The computer confirmed her status, repeated the charge of accessing classified information and said further investigation was necessary.

Jade removed her headset, logged off, and waited. There would be only sixty seconds before the Placators came to take her to the Interrogation Chamber—a small, cell-like room in the Main Block. She had been there once. It had been an innocent mistake, asking Pupil 150 for help, but the punishment had been two foul days on garbage duty.

Precisely sixty seconds later the Training Module doors opened and Jade was taken outside by two expressionless Placators. Once she was inside the Interrogation Chamber the Placators left and the automatic doors closed. Jade was alone with a keyboard and a large screen from which the impassive face of a Zarg stared down at her.

"Key in your personal code and number," said the Zarg.

Anxiety made her fingers tremble slightly as they skimmed the keyboard.

"Code accepted," said the Zarg. "Greetings L42."

Jade breathed a deep sigh of relief. Not only had her mother's code been accepted, it proved that the screen only worked one way. She could not be seen or visually identified.

"Question," said the Zarg. "What are you researching, L42?"

Jade keyed in Rules in Society.

"Reason validated," said the Zarg.

Jade smiled. "Well! That was easier than I thought."

She turned to go, but the IC doors had not opened and the Zarg's unseeing eyes were still staring at her from the screen. There was yet another question.

"What do you think of the Zarg system?"

Jade tried to think what her mother would say. Something sugary and sanitized like … the Zarg system is perfect in every way. She keyed this in but the doors did not open.

"Received information, incorrect."

Jade tried again.

"The Zarg system is supreme. The Zarg system is all-powerful."

Nothing worked and the Zarg began to lose patience. It told L42 to wait while it put a search on the personnel files. Jade's shoulders sagged. To be caught out on such a silly question! Trembling, she covered her face with her hands and at the same moment the strange handwritten words in her grandmother's book came dancing before her eyes.

Vox et praeterea nihil.

She had nothing to lose. Jade keyed in the four mysterious words. The effect on the screen was startling. The Zarg face was suddenly smothered by a vivid display of graphics, static, and scrambled information.

"Obsolete. Unknown," said the Zarg weakly. "Repeat!"

This time words and pictures zapped across the screen in a brainstorm of electronic fury, until with a final and blinding flash the screen blanked out completely.

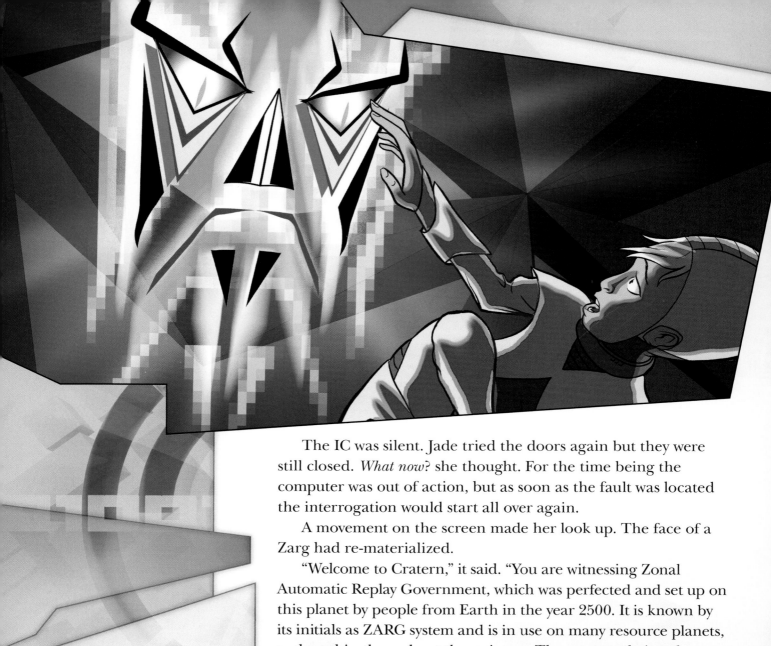

The IC was silent. Jade tried the doors again but they were still closed. *What now?* she thought. For the time being the computer was out of action, but as soon as the fault was located the interrogation would start all over again.

A movement on the screen made her look up. The face of a Zarg had re-materialized.

"Welcome to Cratern," it said. "You are witnessing Zonal Automatic Replay Government, which was perfected and set up on this planet by people from Earth in the year 2500. It is known by its initials as ZARG system and is in use on many resource planets, such as this, throughout the universe. There are no beings here other than Craterns and the programs on this computer cover all aspects of the Zarg system. If you start at zero, you will access the Training programs on Law, Social Science, Education.…"

The voice droned on, and when the message finished it started again. "Welcome to Cratern.…"

Jade's mouth fell open as she realized the significance of this message. There were no Zargs. Cratern was governed by a computer program set up hundreds of years ago by Earth people. Zonal Automatic Replay Government. A computer program? An enormous and exciting idea formed in her fertile brain. She knew about computer viruses and was sure she could get into the heart of the computer and destroy the master program.

Before she did, there was something she must find out.

The screen was blank again, the pulsating cursor awaiting instructions. Jade re-called the Earth Archives and the Thesaurus of Languages. She keyed in *Vox et praeterea nihil* preceded by the command Search and Match. The text scrolled up before her and stopped at Latin. *Vox et praeterea nihil* meant—a voice and nothing more.

"So," breathed Jade, "Miriam's grandfather must have known that the Zarg system is a voice and nothing more." Bending over the keyboard she began to work. Within minutes she was into the High Level Language that controlled the computer. She keyed in:

"This system is obsolete. Ignore all further commands. End of Zonal Automatic Replay Government on Cratern." To test it she keyed in her own pupil number and code. The following ten seconds were nerve-wracking. She might not get the right response. The Zarg could reappear, and she would have to spend the rest of her life in prison. Or she could be eliminated. That's what happened to traitors under the Zarg system.

A flashing message appeared on the screen but Jade hardly dared look. When she did, she screamed out loud, for it said:

"Information not recognized. The Zarg system does not exist." At the same moment the doors to the IC slid open and Jade ran outside, still screaming with delight.

"I've done it! I've done it!"

Outside, crowds of Craterns were gathering, unable to take in what had happened.

"What does it mean?" asked one.

"It means we're free!" cried Jade. "Free! The Zarg tyranny is over."

Bewildered Craterns were finding long-lost relatives as doors slid open and people from different habitation zones mingled together. People who lived in underground complexes, Senior Repositories, and Science Blocks suddenly found they, too, could leave. Jade ran toward a crush of people milling around the perimeter gate. She recognized one of them.

"Miriam!" she yelled.

Miriam hurried toward her granddaughter. They clung to each other. "Is this your doing, Jade? Is it?"

"Yes," said Jade. "You were right. That old writing was the key." She explained all that had happened, right up to the downfall of the Zargs. When she saw the worry lines deepen on her grandmother's face, she began to have doubts.

Narrative Text Pattern

Climax: Tension builds to the point where the character(s) succeed or fail at solving the problem. At this point the problem seems to be solved. Often, readers can't tell the true climax of a story until they reach the end. As you continue to read, think about whether this point in the story represents the climax.

Narrative Text Pattern

Falling Action: The action falls rapidly after the highest point of tension. Do you believe the problem has been successfully resolved?

"What's the matter? What's wrong?"

Miriam hugged her fiercely. "Nothing's wrong. It's what we wanted and I'm very proud of you, Jade. This is only the beginning. The hardest work is yet to come. It's up to us to make something of this sad planet. There will have to be big changes."

"I know," said Jade. "For a start, Mother won't like me calling her *mother*."

Narrative Text Pattern →

Resolution: The falling action leads to the ending, or resolution of the story. This dialogue focuses on the future. How does that help to clearly show that this story has come to an end?

Narrative Text Pattern →

Subplot: Subplots are often resolved at the same time as the main story. How does the author resolve the subplot involving Jade's family?

Miriam chuckled. "She won't like being called Buttercup, either. She never did like her real name."

Reflecting

Understanding Text Patterns: How does the subplot support the main conflict in the story?

Metacognition: Create a diagram to help you understand this story. What other strategies could help you understand this story?

Critical Thinking: What do you think of the idea that a society could be run by computers? How believable is it that the computer system could be shut down so easily?

ACROSS THREE MiLLENNiA

Short Story by Emily Smith

Philip gazed at the abacus in front of him. There was a bit of shade from the fig tree, but even so sweat broke and trickled down his brow. His heart was hammering. Calm down, he told himself fiercely. You've used an abacus before. What was it Cleon had always told his pupils? "The abacus can never lie."

Lalda sat at the console of CMf-22, probably the most powerful computer in the universe. It was soothing to see the lines of green lights across the top of the instrument panel. All functions in order.

Moving a hand to the gleaming instrument panel, she pressed for autocheck—vocal mode. "Autopilot—check!" The tinny voice rang out through the cabin, mechanical, reassuring. "Coordinates log—check! Navigation drive—check! Scanning systems—check!" Lalda breathed a sigh. It was all going to be all right.

Even though Briel had died, and she was now on her own, it was going to be all right.

Philip looked toward the site. A gang of slaves was hard at work digging the foundations. Suddenly, he saw the foreman coming back, with Cimon, the architect. As they neared the fig tree, Philip leapt to his feet. But the architect and foreman took no notice. They turned and carried on their conversation.

"Oh, it will be superb!" Cimon said. "We really are building a temple worthy of Apollo!"

"May he shine forever," murmured the foreman dutifully.

"You know something," Cimon went on in a thoughtful tone, "there's a man back in Athens who's going around saying the Sun is a mass of flaming material."

"Really?" said the foreman, not sounding that interested.

"Mind you, it would be quite something if he was right," the architect went on slowly. "Quite something...."

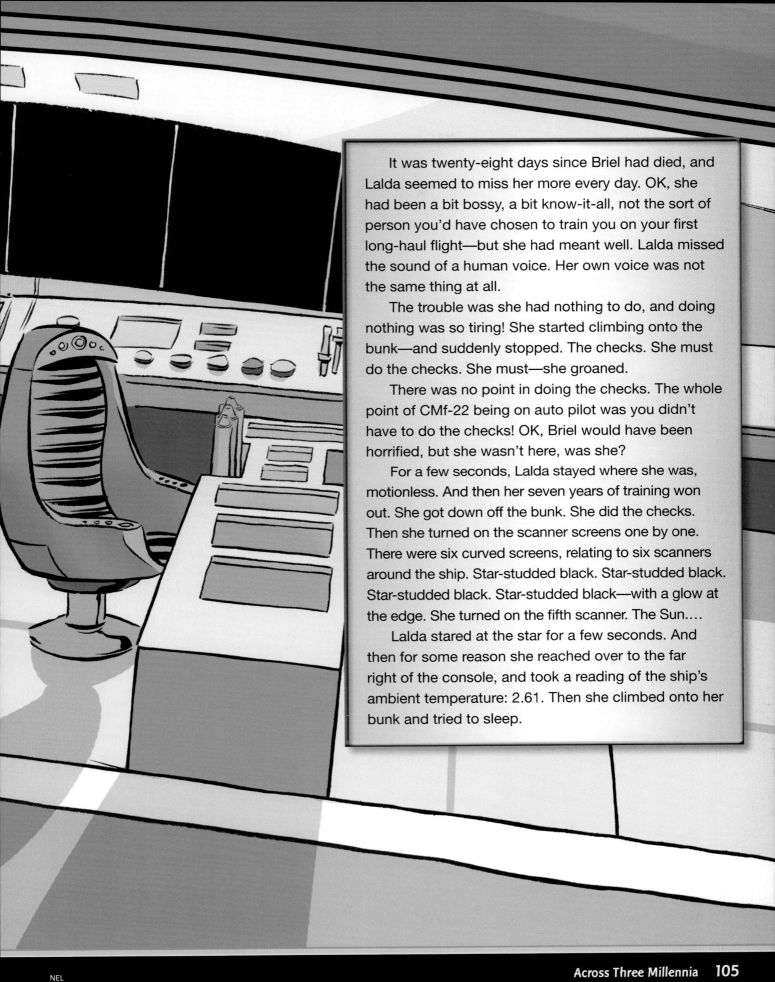

It was twenty-eight days since Briel had died, and Lalda seemed to miss her more every day. OK, she had been a bit bossy, a bit know-it-all, not the sort of person you'd have chosen to train you on your first long-haul flight—but she had meant well. Lalda missed the sound of a human voice. Her own voice was not the same thing at all.

The trouble was she had nothing to do, and doing nothing was so tiring! She started climbing onto the bunk—and suddenly stopped. The checks. She must do the checks. She must—she groaned.

There was no point in doing the checks. The whole point of CMf-22 being on auto pilot was you didn't have to do the checks! OK, Briel would have been horrified, but she wasn't here, was she?

For a few seconds, Lalda stayed where she was, motionless. And then her seven years of training won out. She got down off the bunk. She did the checks. Then she turned on the scanner screens one by one. There were six curved screens, relating to six scanners around the ship. Star-studded black. Star-studded black. Star-studded black. Star-studded black—with a glow at the edge. She turned on the fifth scanner. The Sun….

Lalda stared at the star for a few seconds. And then for some reason she reached over to the far right of the console, and took a reading of the ship's ambient temperature: 2.61. Then she climbed onto her bunk and tried to sleep.

Cimon was looking down at Philip. His brown eyes were keen. "So you're the young man asking for work?"

Philip nodded. "Yes, sir."

Cimon put his scroll on the small table. "I could do with a bright boy. Someone who knows his way around." Cimon narrowed his eyes. "But why should I choose you?"

Because I desperately need the work, and if I don't earn any money soon, my mother and sisters and I will starve. No, don't say that. "Because I—I'll work hard and … and I learn quickly!" Philip stammered.

Cimon turned to the foreman. "You said you knew his family?"

The foreman gave a shrug. "Yeah," he said.

"Good," said Cimon briskly. He turned to Philip. "Well, I should be able to give you a trial. There's only one thing." He reached over and picked up the abacus from the table.

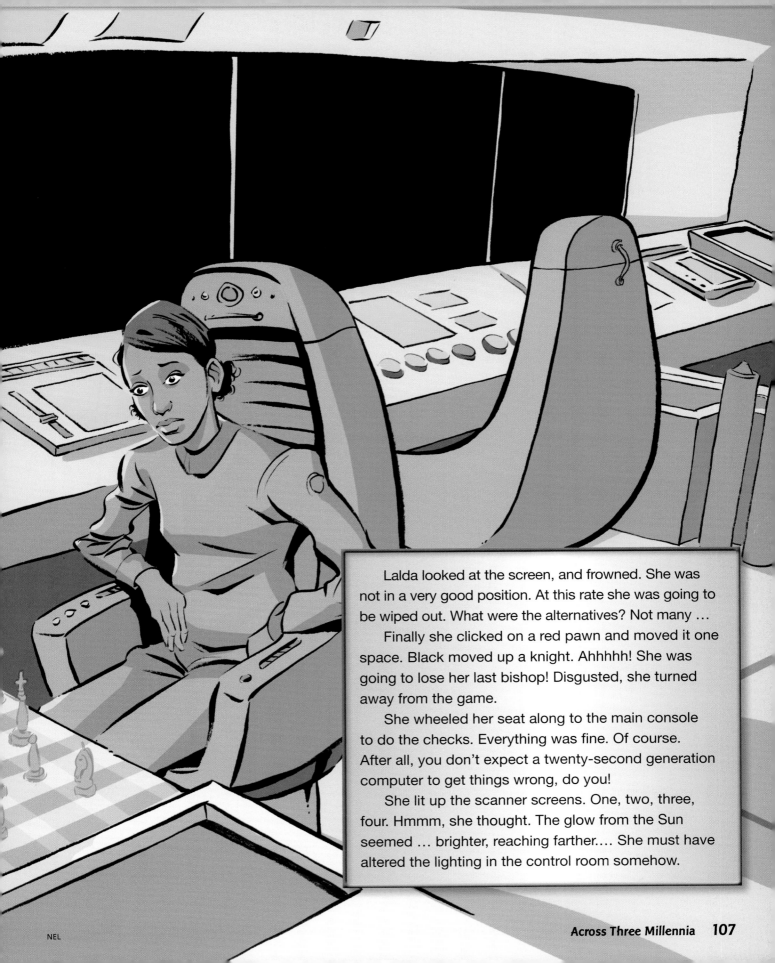

Lalda looked at the screen, and frowned. She was not in a very good position. At this rate she was going to be wiped out. What were the alternatives? Not many …

Finally she clicked on a red pawn and moved it one space. Black moved up a knight. Ahhhhh! She was going to lose her last bishop! Disgusted, she turned away from the game.

She wheeled her seat along to the main console to do the checks. Everything was fine. Of course. After all, you don't expect a twenty-second generation computer to get things wrong, do you!

She lit up the scanner screens. One, two, three, four. Hmmm, she thought. The glow from the Sun seemed … brighter, reaching farther…. She must have altered the lighting in the control room somehow.

With one long finger Cimon spun a bead on the abacus. "I need someone with a head for figures."

Philip tried to look like someone with a head for figures.

"Nothing really complicated, I mean—just basic calculations. You can manage those, can't you?"

"Y-yes!" said Philip.

Cimon put the abacus in his hands. "Let's see what you can do." He unrolled his papyrus scroll. "Now, what shall I ask you …?"

Philip tried to stop the shaking of his hands. Stay calm, he told himself. You can use an abacus. You were old Cleon's best pupil before you had to stop school because of the money.

Cimon's voice broke in. "Add three hundred and fifty and seventy-five."

Lalda poured herself some fruit juice, drank half of it, and started toward the control room, carrying the cup. Suddenly she stopped. What was she doing? No loose liquids in the control room—that was the rule.

Drinkless and back in the control room, she ran her eye over the green lights, then started her checks. "Autopilot—check!" pinged CMf-22. "Coordinates log—check! Navigation drive—check!"

Good old CMf-22, thought Lalda in a sudden rush of gratitude. She didn't have to do a thing until re-entry, and even then the experts on Earth Base would be overseeing operations. They wouldn't take any chances—not with her cargo of 500 000 precious pactiles of lithinium.

She started turning on the scanners. Star-studded black. Star-studded black. Star-studded black. Star-studded black— oh! The glow of the Sun was stronger than ever.

Lalda frowned. She lit up the fifth screen. There it was. The Sun. But something was different. It was … bigger.

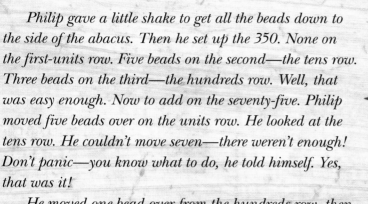

Philip gave a little shake to get all the beads down to the side of the abacus. Then he set up the 350. None on the first-units row. Five beads on the second—the tens row. Three beads on the third—the hundreds row. Well, that was easy enough. Now to add on the seventy-five. Philip moved five beads over on the units row. He looked at the tens row. He couldn't move seven—there weren't enough! Don't panic—you know what to do, he told himself. Yes, that was it!

He moved one bead over from the hundreds row, then three back from the tens row. And read his answer off. "Four hundred and twenty-five!"

Cimon nodded. "That's it. A subtraction now, I think." He scratched his head. His eyes travelled over the papyrus.

Hands shaking, Lalda moved over to get a reading on the ship's ambient temperature. It was 2.84. And it had been 2.61! She sat back in her chair, heart thumping. Surely that meant the ship was moving toward the Sun.

She couldn't believe it. All those checks—and the ship was travelling toward the Sun! She lifted her eyes to the row of lights at the top of the instrument panel. Green, green—every single one of them green!

Suddenly, she launched herself at the console. Her fingers flew on buttons, switches, dials, keyboards. The answers were still the same. As far as CMf-22 was concerned, the ship was on course.

She gritted her teeth. Right. Self-checks on all functions! All operating circuits to be scanned! Self-check program to be left on loop! Memory banks to be scanned for signs of computer malfunction! All flight recordings to be retrieved from data files, and discrepancies entered on screen!

For an hour Lalda worked as she had never worked before. She found nothing. No discrepancies. No signs of malfunction. The ship was on course, and would be docking on Earth in nineteen days. She had panicked unnecessarily. Or had she …?

The Sun was high in the sky now. Philip was vaguely aware that the slaves had stopped for a break. His whole body was tensed, waiting. Subtraction. He prayed that he would be able to do it.

"Ah, here's one." Cimon looked across at him. "Six thousand, take away one thousand, five hundred and fifty-five."

Philip set to work. As he finished the tens line, he frowned. That couldn't be right, surely? What had happened? Suddenly he looked at the units line. Oh, of course! He had to finish the whole sum before the tens line came out right. Thankfully, he moved the last lot of beads. So the abacus was right after all. That's what his teacher Cleon had always been on about. "Four thousand, four hundred and forty-five," he said triumphantly.

The architect nodded, and glanced toward the site. "Last one now. Five thousand take away five."

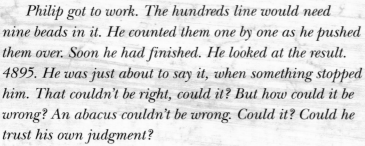

Philip got to work. The hundreds line would need nine beads in it. He counted them one by one as he pushed them over. Soon he had finished. He looked at the result. 4895. He was just about to say it, when something stopped him. That couldn't be right, could it? But how could it be wrong? An abacus couldn't be wrong. Could it? Could he trust his own judgment?

Cimon was waiting for his answer. Philip's head was buzzing.

What was she to do? CMf-22 was telling her everything was OK. All CMf-22's backup and self-check programs were telling her everything was OK. But Lalda knew it wasn't.

And the longer she left it, the worse it would get. The Sun was still millions of kilometres away, but at some stage its radiation would start to affect the ship's functions. She sat back in her seat. Should she override the autopilot, and navigate the ship herself?

On the one hand was CMf-22, probably the most powerful and reliable computer in the known universe. On the other hand was—what? The instincts of an inexperienced space pilot. Should she really trust her own judgment?

Turning her seat sideways, she pressed a button. A curved shutter slid away—disclosing a panel of instruments. Pilot control instruments. She stared at the start-up button.

Lalda made her decision. She pressed the start-up button.

Philip made his decision. "Four, nine, nine, five," he said.

Philip looked down, so as not to meet Cimon's eyes. A vision of his thin, hungry sisters flashed in his mind. And then he stared. For there, by his bare feet, were two bits of green pottery—two halves of the sort of bead you would find on an abacus. His heart leapt. He looked up at Cimon—at his new employer.

The autopilot was on hold. Lalda had all the readings she needed. She was nudging the ship round in an arc. She was beginning to feel confident. Maybe she really could navigate the ship.

There was a beeping noise. She glanced up at the row of lights on the top of the instrument panel. The second light from the end wasn't green any more. It was red. And lit up on its surface were the words, "Autopilot Functions Failure." Her heart leapt. She looked back at the screens—at the world of space that was hers.

Author's Note

The Ancient Greeks—and the Romans—used letters for numerals. These had no place value, so could not be put in columns, which made arithmetic very difficult. An abacus was the best way of doing calculations, until Arabic numerals—and the zero—were developed.

Reflecting

Understanding Text Patterns: What is the conflict in this selection? How is it resolved?

Metacognition: What helps you track both stories simultaneously?

Critical Thinking: How does the layout help you to follow the two separate narratives? How do you respond differently to each narrative?

The reading strategy you learned in this unit can help you to better understand text in other subject areas as well as in the real world. Think about the questions you would ask yourself as you read this article and reflect on its statistics.

School Assignments on the Internet

Informational Article from Young Canadians in a Wired World Phase II

In 2005, the Media Awareness Network surveyed more than 5000 Canadian students in Grades 4 to 11. Students represented each province and territory, English- and French-language schools, and urban and rural environments. The following article shows some of the survey results.

Students were asked: "How often do you use the Internet for school assignments?" (Figure 1) The proportion who "almost never" do online assignments drops from Grade 4 to Grade 7, then levels off. About one-third in each grade do online assignments "a few times a month." The proportion who do online assignments "once or twice a week" increases to about one-third of students in Grade 11. The proportion who do online assignments "more than twice a week" increases up to Grade 8, then recedes through the high school years. By Grade 11 it is back to the Grade 5 level.

FIGURE 1 *How often do you use the Internet for school assignments?*

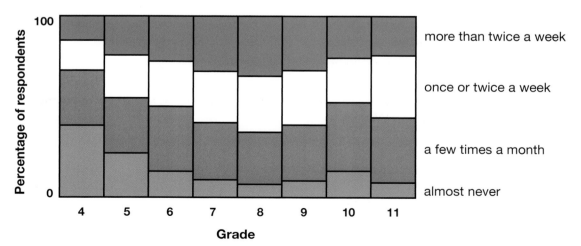

Students were asked whether they would prefer to get information for school assignments from books in a library or from the Internet. The Internet is the clear winner (Figure 2), and it is not hard to imagine reasons for the choice. The Net is convenient and fast.

FIGURE 2 **How do you prefer to get information for school assignments?**
Source: *YCWW II, 2005*

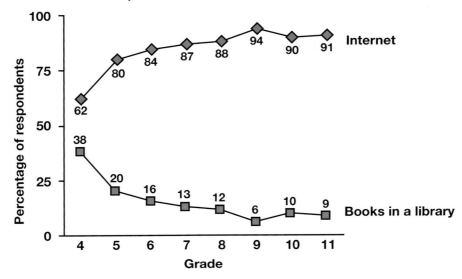

In Grade 4 the preference for online research is already well established, with 62% favouring the online method and 38% preferring to get information from books in a library. The preference for the Internet climbs rapidly to Grades 5 and 6 and then more slowly. This trend mirrors kids' adoption of the Internet as a tool for doing homework.

For most, the Internet is an enjoyable way to do school work: 58% of students say they like the Net for school work, while only 15% say that they dislike it. There are not meaningful differences in response to this question on the basis of grade, gender, or geographical location.

FIGURE 3 **Does the Net make any difference to the quality of your school work?**
YCWW II, 2005

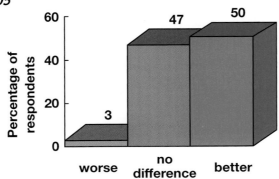

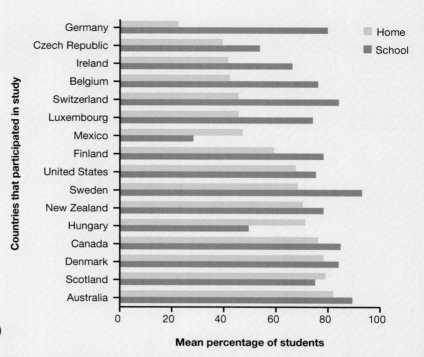

FIGURE 4 *Global availability of the use of computers for 15-year-olds at home and school*

Mean percentage of 15-year-olds who reported having a computer available to use

Source: Data from Programme for International Student Assessment (PISA)

Canada, Australia, Finland, Iceland, and Luxembourg all had high rates of school connectivity, with 80% or more of their school computers online. Although the United States had a high number of students per computer, only 39% of their school computers were connected to the Internet.

How Valuable Is Internet Research?

Some experts are concerned about the value of online research. One Montréal teacher visited over 40 schools investigating how the Internet was used. He observed over 1000 students. Students flipped from site to site—on average 15 to 25 times per hour. They were often unable to respond comprehensively or critically to the sites they visited. He concluded that most students don't absorb anything of value during Internet research.

Reflecting

Questioning: What type of questions did you ask as you read this selection and examined the charts and graphs?

Metacognition: How did the charts and graphs help you understand the text? How did the text help you understand the charts and graphs?

Critical Literacy: What questions did the selection ignore or overlook?

Selections Grouped by Theme and Form

Index

Credits

Text

3–5 "Global Citizens" (p. 4) and "What Is a Global Issue?" (pp. 20–21) from *Being Active Citizens* by Sue Watson, Macmillan Education Australia, 2003. Copyright © Susan Watson, 2003. Reproduced by permission of Macmillan Education Australia. 6–7 "Globalization" from *Globalization* by Iris Teichmann first published in the UK by Franklin Watts, a division of The Watts Publishing Group Ltd., 338 Euston Road, London NW1 3BH. 8–11 Tips designed by various artists from *Change the World for Ten Bucks*. Reprinted with permission from the publisher. 12–20 *Two Islands* by Ivan Gantschev © 1985 by NorthSouth Books Inc., New York. 21 "Who Made a Mess?" from *The Day I Fell Down the Toilet* by Steve Turner (Lion Publishing, 1996), copyright © Steve Turner 1996, reprinted by permission of the publisher. 22 "Timesweep" from HONEY AND SALT, copyright © 1963 by Carl Sandburg and renewed 1991 by Margaret Sandburg, Helga Sandburg Crile and Janet Sandburg, reprinted by permission of Houghton Mifflin Harcourt Publishing Company. 23 "I'd Like to Squeeze" copyright © 1996 by John Agard, reproduced by kind permission of John Agard c/o Caroline Sheldon Literary Agency Limited. 25–26 Reprinted with permission, Torstar Syndication Services. 27–29 "What Is Child Labor?" From FACES April 2006 issue: Kids At Work. © 2006, Carus Publishing Company, published by Cobblestone Publishing, 30 Grove Street, Suite C, Peterborough, NH 03458. All Rights Reserved. Used by permission of the publisher. 30–31 *Child Slavery in Modern Times* by Shirlee P. Newman. © 2000 Franklin Watts, a Division of Grolier Publishing, Inc. All rights reserved. Reprinted by permission of Franklin Watts, an imprint of Scholastic Library Publishing, Inc. 33–35 Text and photographs courtesy The Historica Foundation of Canada. 36–37 "Who Owns the Land?" from *Tales for an Unknown City*, collected by Dan Yashinsky (p. 14.) McGill-Queen's University Press, 1990. 40 Advertisement Courtesy Global Vision International. 41 Advertisement Courtesy Youth Challenge International. 43–45 ©Peter Menzel/ from the book *Hungry Planet: What the World Eats*, by Peter Menzel and Faith D'Aluisio. 47–50 Reprinted courtesy of Doctors Without Borders/Médicins Sans Frontières (MSF). 51–53 "Art, Politics and Questioning Authority," by Ilona Dougherty, from *Notes From Canada's Young Activists*, edited by Severn Cullis-Suzuki, published 2007 by Greystone Books, a division of Douglas & McIntyre Ltd. Reprinted by permission of the publisher. 54–56 From DRAPER ET AL. *Gage Human Geography 8*. © 2000 Nelson Education Ltd. Reproduced by permission. www.cengage.com/permissions. 59–61 From *Risk Takers and Innovators* by Sandra Phinney, 2004. Reprinted with permission from James Lorimer and Company Limited. 62–63 "Rubber Shortage Leads to Silly Putty," adapted chapter of "Silly Putty" from *TOYS! Amazing Stories Behind Some Great Inventions* by Don Wulffson. Copyright © 2000 Don L. Wulffson. Reprinted by permission of Henry Holt and Company, LLC. 64 "Light Bulb," from FLICKER FLASH by Joan Bransfield Graham. Text copyright © by Joan Bransfield Graham. Reprinted by permission of Houghton Mifflin Harcourt Publishing Company. All rights reserved. 65 Used with permission from Michelle Muir. 66–69 Excerpt from *Canadian Inventors*. Text copyright © 2004 by Maxine Trottier. Reproduced by permission of Scholastic Canada. 74–75 Extract from *Would You Believe . . . cobwebs stop wounds bleeding? And other medical marvels* by Richard Platt (OUP, 2006), copyright © Oxford University Press 2006, reprinted by permission of Oxford University Press. 81–83 Reprinted by permission of Cricket Magazine Group, Carus Publishing Company from ASK magazine September 2006, Vol. 6, No. 7, English text copyright © 2007 by Richard Young. French language version with permission from Richard Young. 86 ZITS © ZITS PARTNERSHIP, KING FEATURES SYNDICATE. 87 SHERMAN'S LAGOON © JIM TOOMEY, KING FEATURES SYNDICATE. 88 Julian S. Krupa. 90–91 Reprinted by permission of Cricket Magazine Group, Carus Publishing Company from ASK magazine July/August 2007, Vol. 6, No. 6, copyright © 2007 by Carus Publishing Company. 93–102 "The Zarg Tyranny" by Valerie Thame. Reprinted with permission from Orion Children's Books. 103–113 "Across Three Millennia" by Emily Smith from *Sensational Cyber Stories*/collected by Tony Bradman, 1997. 114–116 Reprinted with permission from Media Awareness Network; (Figure 4) Adapted from Statistics Canada, http://www.statcan.ca/english/edu/feature/computer.htm, last modified on 2005-03-07; "How Valuable is Internet Research" adapted from the UNESCO Courier, March 2001.

Photos

Cover: (globe face) Perrush/Shutterstock; (blue burst) Shane Thomas Shaw/Shutterstock; (freeway) Chistoprudov Dmitriy Gennadievich/Shutterstock; (paper) IKO/Shutterstock; (cyborg) ©iStockphoto.com/Konstantin Inozemtsev. 1 (silhouette) Galyna Andrushko/Shutterstock; (Earth) Frank Boston/Shutterstock. 2 Yukmin/Getty Images. 3–7 (Background trees) PKruger/Shutterstock. 3 (African woman) Lucian Coman/Shutterstock; (boy in Turkish headdress) Christopher Furlong/Getty Images; (Asian girl) Hugo Maes/Shutterstock; (Earth) Serp/Shutterstock. 4 (shoreline with fish) Doug Menuez/Getty Images; (protesters with sign) Manpreet Romana/AFP/Getty Images; (men in canoes) Jose Gil/Shutterstock. 5 (solar panel) Otmar Smit/Shutterstock; (L'Anse aux Meadows) © All Canada Photos/Alamy; (homeless man) emin kuliyev/Shutterstock. 6 China Photos/Getty Images. 7 Paul Bronstein/Getty Images. 10 (photo only) © Stepanov/Dreamstime.com. 11 (photo only) Paul Schutzer/Time Life Pictures/Getty Images. 21–23 (city) Laurin Rinder/Shutterstock. 21 (stumps) Marinko Tarlac/Shutterstock; (desert) Galyna Andrushko/Shutterstock; (globe) Frank Boston Shutterstock. 22–23 (crowd) Andrija Kova/Shutterstock; (family) iofoto/Shutterstock. 23 (hands) Andrew Cribb/Shutterstock. 24 © Bob Daemmrich/PhotoEdit Inc. 25 David Cooper/Toronto Star; 25–26 (doves) Tomas Smolek/Shutterstock; (newspaper background) © iStockphoto.com/Christine Balderas. 27 P. Lissac/ILO. 28 AP Photo/K.M. Choudary. 29 (boy and girl on rubble) © Roger Arnold; (girl picking cotton) © Reza Websitan/CORBIS; (child welding) Ruby/Alamy. 30–31 (protesters) morgan mansour/Shutterstock; (brick wall) charles taylor/Shutterstock. 30 John Van Hasselt/CORBIS SYGMA. 31 © Tom Craig/Alamy. 32 © Corbis Premium RF/Alamy. 33–35 Lucille Teasdale photos courtesy The Historica Foundation of Canada; (Uganda scenery) © iStockphoto.com/andydidyk; (cardstock) © iStockphoto.com/Bill Noll; (sign) © iStockphoto.com/Jane Norton. 36–37 Terrance Emerson/Shutterstock. 38 (photo only on cover of FACES) © blickwinkel/Alamy. 39 Cover of *Change the World for Ten Bucks* reprinted with permission from We Are What We Do. 40–41 (palm trees) HP_Photo/Shutterstock; (baobabs) Muriel Lasure/Shutterstock; (airplane) sabri deniz kizil/Shutterstock. 41 (girl) Yuri Arcurs/Shutterstock; (compass) In-Finity/Shutterstock; (Earth) Michael D. Brown/Shutterstock; (rhino) Johan Swanepoel/Shutterstock. 43–45 (all) ©Peter Menzel/ from the book *Hungry Planet: What the World Eats*, by Peter Menzel and Faith D'Aluisio. 47 Andrew Cabeller-Reynolds/Getty Images. 50 Jean-Marc Gibour/Getty Images. 51–52 (male) Agb/Shutterstock; (female) Telnov Olenskii/Shutterstock. 53 vanias/Shutterstock. 54 Marcus Brown/Shutterstock. 56 Adisa/Shutterstock. 57 (background) Kheng Guan Toh/Shutterstock; (cell phone) Elnur/Shutterstock; (old phone) Scott Rothstein/Shutterstock. 58 © Michael Newman/Photoedit. 59–61 salamanderman/Shutterstock. 59 (plastic bottle) 6454881632/Shutterstock. 60 & 61 Courtesy of Gina Gallant. 62–63 (bubbles) suravid/Shutterstock. 62 Igor Smichkov/Shutterstock. 63 Valkr/Shutterstock. 64 Image Club. 65 Gunpreet/Shutterstock. 66, 68, and 69 Photos courtesy of the Zimmerman Family. 66–69 (background) sgame/Shutterstock; Kim D. French/Shutterstock. 70 Anyka/Shutterstock. 71 (television) Palto/Shutterstock; (cityscape) Antonis Papantoniou/Shutterstock; (car) Computer Earth/Shutterstock. 72 I. Glory/Alamy. 74 (pillar) Réunion des Musées Nationaux/Art Resource, NY; (lizard) Dr. Morley Read/Shutterstock. (sesame seeds) travis manley/Shutterstock; (figs) Moiseeva Galina Gavrilovna/Shutterstock; (laurel) Tina Rencelj/Shutterstock. 75 (sitting dog sculpture) Erich Lessing/Art Resource NY; (apples) Elnur/Shutterstock; (resin) Pontus Edenberg/Shutterstock; (mint) Eric Gevaert/Shutterstock. 76 (boy) Chris Clinton/Getty Images. 77–78 (woman at computer) PhotoCreate/Shutterstock; (nanotubes) © iStockphoto.com/Martin McCarthy. 78 (medication) © iStockphoto.com/Daniel Kourey. 79 (surgery) © iStockphoto.com/Jacob Wackerhousen. 80 © Will Hart/Photo Edit. 81–83 (background) SSilver/Shutterstock; (cyborg images) © iStockphoto.com/Konstantin Inezemtsev; 84–85 (circuitboard) coko/Shutterstock; (steel arms) Sebastian Kaulitzki. 88–89 © iStockphoto.com/Benjamin Goode. 92 © Michael Newman/Photo Edit. 93–102 Phecsone/Shutterstock. 103–113 (papyrus) Najin/Shutterstock; (sun) CnAp Tak/Shutterstock.

Art

48–49 map by Deborah Crowle. 89 illustrated by Christopher Short. 93–102 illustrated by Marcelo Baez. 103–113 illustrated by Kagan McLeod.